Donia

Her Bravery, Her Luck
and
Her Challenging Destiny

Shlomo Adler

ISBN 978-0-9801250-7-8

Acknowledgments
From the Author, Shlomo Adler

Special thanks to my friend from my childhood, Jack Greene of Sydney, Australia, for convincing me to translate this book into English and for supporting it financially.

And to all those who encouraged and financially supported the publication of this book: Mr. Israel Kass, Volvo Honda importer, Israel; Mr. Hugo Marom, aviation consultant; Mr. Samuel Rainhartz (Malka's son).

Thanks to everyone who helped find historical material and data relating to the villages of Synowódzko Niżne and Wyżne and the towns of Stryj and Bolechów: Mr. Victor Prystai, Mr. Matthew Yaari (Wald), The Association of Stryj in Israel, Mr. Sanko Taras Ivanovicz.

Mrs. Dina Ostrower, "Donia," who agreed to leave anonymity and tell me this heroic and unique story.

Jacob Ostrower, Dina's son, for convincing his mother to allow her story to be told and for his help during its writing.

Mrs. Malka (Miriam) Rainhartz, B.M for her cooperation and her stories from before the war, about hiding during the Holocaust and after the liberation. (She passed away during the summer of 2015.)

My son David who traveled with me to all these places, photographed them and supported me in every way.

An unknown lady from Synowódzko Niżne for helping find links to people and who recommended sites that deserved to be photographed.

Messrs. Bogdan Matloch from Bolechów and Miron

Hoshovsky from Gerynia village for their help locating the building that served as the German casino in Bolechów during the Holocaust. (Both gentlemen have since passed away)

Mr. Igor Czopko for his help collecting materials.

Mrs. Francine Slivka for her help in the first translation from my poor vocabulary to English.

Mrs. Joan Adler for her help in the final translation and editing of this book.

My wife Esther for allowing me to change my study into a "Center of Galicia" for my books and other activities.

A Note from the Editor, Joan Adler

It has been my honor to work with Shlomo Adler to translate *Donia* into Englsh. English is not Shlomo's native language, nor is it his second or even third language.

I have tried to preserve exactly what he was communicating without changing the essence of his writing. One will notice that the story is told in the voice of someone who is not a native English speaker. This is intentional. I felt it would give the reader the true "feel" of the story as told by the author.

In many cases the names of the towns mentioned in this book have changed since the end of World War II. The author refers to these towns by the name he (and Donia) knew from their childhood.

Acknowledgments
From Donia's son, Jacob Ostrower

The first person who deserves gratitude and blessings is the author, Shlomo Adler, who wrote this book. This is his second book. For many years he has devoted his time to the research and documentation of the Holocaust. He wrote this book, as told to him directly by Donia, with patience and exceptional sensitivity while still being certain that all facts were accurate. It expands our knowledge of the history of the period and events.

Donia's heroic actions, in particular, give the book added value and enable both the enrichment of the knowledge and understanding of the events during this period as we marvel at the extraordinary heroic story of Donia.

Thanks to Mrs. Miriam Rainhartz B.M for her support, encouragement and extensive assistance with details and information of the events of the period from the time of her stay in hiding with her late husband Shlomo Siumek Rainhartz.

Blessing to the Hebrew linguistic editor of the book, Mr. Simon Bouzaglo.

Finally blessing to my mother Dina/Donia (Pikholtz) Ostrower who agreed, after more than 60 years, to bring her story to the public, devoting her time and force for the publishing of her amazing story.

Table of Contents

List of Photographs and Ilustrations

Introduction

This book is based on real events in the life of the heroine. The author received her approval to write about them.

Years ago I heard the story of the miraculous rescue in Bolechów of Siumek (Shlomo) and Malka (Miriam) Rainhartz by a Ukrainian girl. After the liberation, the Ukrainian girl revealed her true identity as that of a Jew born in the village of Synowódzko Niżne located over the mountains not far from my hometown, Bolechów. The girl saved herself and a Jewish couple with courage, ingenuity and luck. She challenged fate using fake Aryan papers.

When, in 1994, I began documenting the Holocaust by filling out Pages of Testimony for Yad Vashem and writing my memoirs, I asked the Rainhartzes a number of times to give me the name and address of their savior. I wanted to get the full testimony and the story of the courageous stand she chose. I was convinced that Donia's story should be told; to set as an example of resourcefulness and bravery for future generations.

Mr. and Mrs. Rainhartz would always say, "The woman wants to remain anonymous. She is not looking for fame."

Shlomo and Malka Rainhartz's rescue story was known and told but not in detail in books by Anatole Reginier, *Damals in Bolechów*, published by Bertelsman Germany; in *The Town Square is Empty*, by Yad Vashem Jerusalem; in Daniel Mendelsohn's book, *The Lost;* and in my book, *I am a Jew Again*, published by Yad Vashem.

Who saved them was not known until now. She is Jewish but does not want to talk about it and wants to remain anonymous.

"Please there is no reason for you to create a relationship with her," the Rainhartzes always said.

Apparently, this couple was not eager to talk about their experience although they spoke briefly to several authors who drafted the story. No further details were given.

Shlomo Rainhartz passed away several years ago. Malka (Miriam), his wife, was still living in Beersheba, Israel and I was in touch with her. Unfortunately she recently passed away. May her soul be blessed.

About a year and a half ago I happened to speak with Malka's daughter and this is how I learned that Donia's husband Joseph had died.

"Who is Donia?" I asked.

"The woman who rescued my parents," she replied.

I asked her to give me Donia's phone number so that I could contact her. I wanted to tell her I was sorry for her loss.

Malka's daughter gave me Donia's phone number (as they continued to call her). That is how I learned who the Ukrainian, Dina Ostrower, was.

I called. At the other end of the line I heard a pleasant, relaxed woman's voice. I introduced myself and realized I was talking to Mrs. Ostrower herself. I was not expecting this direct encounter. I thought the receiver would be picked up by someone else in the house.

For years I wanted to speak with this courageous woman who, in my mind, I was comparing to the family who saved me. The feats she accomplished were absolutely comparable to that of my rescuers. And here I was, talking directly with this courageous woman.

First I wanted to offer my condolences to her over her husband's death. I opened the conversation by telling her that for years I had longed to meet her and to hear her go into the details of her story.

I was surprised to learn that Donia knew of me. She would come with the Rainhartz couple to the memorial services I have been organizing over the years for those from Bolechów and the neighborhood that perished in the Holocaust. I naively thought that if the woman was interested in memorials in which the main theme was the Holocaust, I could try to ask her to provide testimony.

I asked her to allow me to interview her so that her story would be heard and would be taught to the younger generation and would remain forever in libraries and archives.

Donia refused saying: "I don't have anything to tell. What I did was just to quiet my tormented conscience because I was the only one in my family to survive."

I spoke with Donia for half an hour using all the arguments at my disposal. I told her that her testimony would be given to Yad Vashem and that it would remain in their archives for research and study. This did not move Donia.

I suggested that I could send her testimony to a film maker and maybe write a book that would be read by thousands of people here and abroad. Nothing convinced her. Donia kept refusing.

I told her, "I will leave you my phone number. If you change your mind, contact me. I would love to hear your story and to write the details."

About two months after my conversation with Donia, in early November 2008, my home phone rang. Donia was on the line. "Mr. Adler," she said. "I'm getting old. My sons ask that my story become known and not remain in the dark. As long as I can trust my memory, I am ready to tell you my story."

It was the day before I was to leave on a two week vacation. I promised I would contact her when I returned, and I did.

I interviewed Donia for about six hours. I was equipped with a tape recorder. Then there were countless phone calls to complete the story and clarify one thing or another.

Donia's story amazed me so much that I gave up writing my second book and devoted myself to writing the story of Donia.

Bolechów, a small town in the foothills of the Carpathian Mountains in Eastern Galicia was, for generations, a stage of events. Governments occasionally passed from hand to hand. The "education" movement flourished in this region in its early years. The pioneers who established the *kibbutzim* in the Israeli valley, the *Merhavia* and others, were trained in agriculture in this region.

The Jews lived together with the extreme Ukrainian nationalists who were teaching the Poles to hate the Jews. The Poles eagerly learned the lesson and waited, ready to practice it. The Poles probably didn't know in those times that the hatred of the Ukrainians towards them was no less than that demonstrated toward the Jews.

After such conviction and wild hatred for the Jews it is no wonder that, out of a population that numbered more than 7,000 Jews in the town and surrounding area, there were only 48 survivors, each with a story and a heroic rescue.

During the memorial events that I organized for the victims of the Holocaust, I used to see a nice looking, blue eyed woman who came with the couple from Beersheba. I was always busy during the memorial events and did not make contact, not even to introduce myself.

When finally I came to her home in Ramat Gan, I met that lovely black-haired, blue eyed woman. In spite her age, the years of suffering, the years she dedicated to her husband who had recently died, she remained a beautiful woman; lucid and young spirited.

On the wall of her living room multiple certificates were hanging. The first and most prominent was:

Certificate I:
Certificate of Registration in the Golden Book
of the Jewish National Fund.
Dina nee Pikholtz

Magnanimous
She, in a perilous situation during the Holocaust, was
courageous and saved two lives
All who saves one life is considered as one
who saved the entire world
Recorded by
Rainhartz, Miriam & Shlomo

Certificate II:
Chai (18) trees
Jerusalem Forest
The name
Dina Ostrower nee Pikholtz
Gave us our lives as gifts.
Rainhartz, Miriam & Shlomo

Certificate III:
Chai (18) trees
Jerusalem Forest
The name
Joseph Ostrower
Dina's faithful husband
In recognition and appreciation
Rainhartz, Miriam & Shlomo

Chai = 18 in Hebrew, is a lucky number,
meaning life

At the beginning Donia said: "I did it for my soul and to ease my conscience. My life had no value, having lost everyone. So I decided that if I had to stay alive, out of my entire extended family, saving this couple will compensate for that. Now, at an advanced age, when I still remember most of it, I want to keep my story as the evidence that human nature may roll down the drain, or alternatively rise to unexpected levels."

For many years, Donia remained secretive. She did not tell anyone what had happened to her during the Holocaust: the hard work in the leather factory, the sad farewell to her entire family on the way to Bełżec, the jumping from the train that was taking every one to their death in Bełżec, the loss of her entire family, and her amazing act of heroism. Donia requested of those she saved not "to tell" in order to remain anonymous.

Her partner of this heroism, Maryjka, originally named Frydka, decided afterward to renounce her Judiasm. Two days after their liberation by the Red Army and the mutual discovery of their Jewish identity, they separated. Fridka went back to Kolczyce village near the town of Sambor and nobody heard from her again.

Anonymous Righteous Among the Nations

After the liberation and recovery, Donia also wanted to return to her village, Synowódzko Niżne to see if a miracle had happened and perhaps someone from her family was saved. In the Stryj train station Donia met an old acquaintance, the conductor, a Polish man, Mr. Pulsa. She knew him before the war because every day she took the train going to school in Stryj.

Pulsa recognized her and told her what the Ukrainian neighbors did to the Jews living in their village before gathering them in the Stryj ghetto.

After hearing what conductor Pulsa said, Donia didn't go to the village. She found that in Stryj, not one single person of her large family had survived. Donia went searching in Sambor where her father's brother, Chaim Pikholtz and his family used to live. Not one of them remained.

In order to be near Sambor, Donia stayed there until the summer of 1945. She worked in a restaurant. When she finally realized that no one from her huge family survived, Donia decided to go with the Jewish youth movement, *Noham*, through Kraków and Bytom. Donia remained in Bytom for several months.

The house of the conductor Pulsa

Later, in December 1945, she moved to Czechosłovakia through forests and mountains along with other members of her youth group. About a week later they moved from Czechosłovakia to a displaced persons camp in Laibhaim, Germany.

After a year in the DP camp, her whole group moved to Italy, to the Arona town on the shore of Lake Maggiore where they lived in a luxurious villa named Verrazano. From Lake Maggiore, they were transported by bus to Venice. From Venice they were taken by boat, in groups of 25-30 people, to the island of Palestrina where they boarded an illegal immigrant ship "*Kadima*" (Forward) together with 794 other people.

Donia could not disembark in the motherland. Along with the other passengers on the "*Kadima*," the British deported her and imprisoned her in a camp on Cyprus for many months. She finally arrived in Israel in 1949 where Donia married her husband Joseph who she'd met in Cyprus.

When I started to write the story of Donia hiding the Rainhartz family, I thought that, as one who himself survived the Holocaust and remained in hiding for a year, I could easily get into Donia's and Malka's skin, and so it was. Often I began to think like them. I was able to understand what they went through and describe their feelings. In order to be really and thoroughly authentic in all that I added to the story of the two elderly women, I even went to Donia's village of Synowódzko Niżne in August 2009.

Background

"Jump my child. Maybe, thanks to you, there will remain a trace and memory of our family." Those were the last words Donia heard from her father. She was a 17 1/2 year old girl before she jumped into the unknown from the train that led her, her immediate family, and thousands of Jews from Stryj and the surrounding villages captured in the *Great Aktion II* to the extermination camp at Bełżec.

Donia was a resourceful girl, and some said even playful. Sometimes the women in the village would say she was a boy who was mistakenly born a girl. Although she wasn't an adult, she relentlessly smuggled skins during the Soviet occupation from 1939 to 1941 to help support her family. To do this she would go to Lwów three times a week pretending to be a student.

During this fateful trip, in a crowded and stuffy car that led them to their deaths at Bełżec, she felt she had to find a way out. Her parents, her brothers and sisters were hysterical and desperate. She stayed calm in order to live.

It was pitch dark inside the car. There was hardly any light at all outside. Donia slowly made her way to the window from which other youngsters had removed the barbed wire. Someone's hands lifted her so that her body was outside the car. The train took a bend slowly. Donia gasped and jumped.

She landed on soft soil. Straw residue remaining from the harvest softened her fall. Beside a number of broken teeth causing severe swelling to her face, she broke no bones nor were any other parts of her body damaged when she landed on the ground. She passed out and has no idea how long she stayed there.

As a child, I heard the name Synowódzko. I knew it was a place not far from the town where I was born and that my grandmother occasionally went there in order to visit her cousins and other relatives.

Other times, when this name was mentioned again, it was during the Holocaust. It was more than a year since my grandmother had been murdered and my parents were no longer with me. I found myself working in the barrel factory. Near us there was a large sawmill where Jews were employed.

I heard the name Synowódzko as a place where Jews were working at a sawmill called Skole2. I also heard it from individual Jews who came from that place and were working in Bolechów in "Delta" or "Hobag," or the " Supreme," big sawmills or in the factory manufacturing barrels. It might be that some of them were in the same labor camp where I was.

At that time I had to fight to survive and I didn't care then. It didn't interest me to know where Synowódzko was and who my grandmother had visited.

This puzzle was solved around the year 2000, when the phone rang at my home in Kfar Saba in Israel and on the line was Mrs. Susan Turnbull from Washington DC. She introduced herself as my relative through my grandmother Bertha (Balcia) Adlersberg, my father's mother. My grandmother was going to visit a sister, the daughter of Mendel Adlersberg from Synowódzko.

Close to my birthplace, Bolechów, there are many villages and small towns. Jews lived in all of them in the past. I went visiting people with my mother - bless her memory. There was an uncle or an aunt. But as a child I never really found out who they were, nor did I care.

I knew a bit more after the conversation with my new cousin Susan. She found me thanks to the many Pages of Testimony I filled out for Yad Vashem. Now I became interested in the place Synowódzko I'd heard of as a child.

After Susan sent me her family tree, I knew a bit more about who was living in Synowódzko. I discovered that there are two places called Synowódzko. One village, Synowódzko Niżne, (Lower Synowódzko) and one Synowódzko Wyżne, (Upper Synowódzko) where there was a large sawmill that belonged to

Mendel Adlersberg, the father of my grandmother Bertha. My grandmother used to go there to visit her sisters, brothers and other siblings.

The Region

The Opir River, as it is named today, starts flowing in the Bojki country. This is where we find the inhabitants of the Beskidy Mountains, in the area known as Tucholszczyzna, near Oporzec and Ławoczne, not far from the former Czech border.

The waters of the Opir River cascade wildly down the mountains. They carry with them bits of mud and rocks. In spring the Opir River is really dangerous. The wild waters wash away bushes and trees growing on the banks of the river. Farmers were afraid to cross the river when the water was overflowing its banks. The river flows near the small towns of Slawsko, Tuchla, Hrebenów and Skole. In the area of Hrebenów, before the Opir River merges with the Stryj River, the water becomes clean and the trout fish taste best compared to those of the Prut and Świca Rivers. In Synowódzko Wyżne the waters of the Opir merge with those of the Stryj.

The Stryj River

The village is situated between two rivers overflowing into an expanding valley. The Opir River creates a large delta that substantially broadens the Stryj River.

This large village was not just the subject of my trip. I mention it because it was the source for the trout supply for restaurants in Bolechów. It was also the place where some cousins and siblings of my grandmother lived. The big sawmill offered work to most of the Synowódzko Wyżne villagers as well as some people from "Synowódzko Niżne." This village was the reason for my trip.

This pastoral village is situated on both sides of the road leading southwest from the Galician town of Stryj through the town of Skole and beyond the Carpathian Mountains province, once the Czech Republic, today Za Karpatie, (over the Carpathian) and on to Hungary.

I travelled to the village of Synowódzko Niżne on a summer day in August 2009 in the company of my son David and Ukrainian Viktor Prystay, "a close" relative through his marriage to the daughter of my rescuers.

My son and I slept in the house of the descendants of my rescuers in the village of Gerynia. It was located between the famous Ukrainian village of Hoshiv and Bolechów, my home town.

We left the village. Roads in this area have not been repaired in decades. There is a one kilometer section paved in huge concrete slabs with a gap of 1.5 inches between them that prevents a smooth ride. We laughed. It probably reminded private car owners of the difference between driving and flying. Probably the factories that manufacture shock absorbers for cars prohibit repairing this stretch of road. All of western Ukraine has very bad roads and owners of cars must replace the shock absorbers in their cars at least once a year.

The distance from the village of Gerynia to the village of Synowódzko Niżne is, as the crow flies, about 12-13 kilometers. Even on foot through the mountain and a place called Bubniszcze, the seat of the legendary bandit Dobosz, the distance does not exceed 20-25 kilometers. But such a walk may be more suitable for young people, and not someone like me, leaning on a cane, and approaching the age of eighty.

The distance on the highway is about 45 kilometers. Viktor

volunteered to take me there.

We passed through my hometown of Bolechów. We drove past the place where the last slave labor camp of the Bolechów Jews and its outlying buildings was located.

We passed the area where the homes of my family stood. And we passed the junction to the train station where I last saw my mother and father as they were transported to an unknown destination.

Then we passed the *Tarbut* school building where I attended school as a child and the canal in which we used to swim and celebrate *Tashlich* ceremonies. We passed the town square, the *rynek*, empty and so different, standing beside the neglected and decaying, impressive synagogue building, The Great Synagogue, as we used to call it. We passed the bridge over the Sukiel River, the crossroad to the village of Luszki and Wołoska Wieś. And we passed the road toward Taniava Forest, a sad reminder of the events of the Holocaust as this is where a mass grave for the Jews of Bolechów is located.

The road winds north through Mount Bolechów and Imperial Oak (Kaiser Aiche), through the villages of Lisowice, a spa named Morszyn and the villages of Dołhe and Stanków.

On the way we encountered a Ukrainian religious procession. People were walking with flags and accompanied by priests on their way to a holy place, the monastery on Mount Hoshiv not far from Gerynia village. They'd left two days before from Lwów . They covered the hundred and fifteen kilometer walk in three days. When they arrived at the foot of the mountain, which has a monastery on its top, the Ukrainians, sinners, or those who have taken a vow, knelt and, as a way of castigation, crawled up to the craggy top. Other participants were waving their flags up toward the sky while loudly singing. As they passed near us I noticed their religious passion.

In Stryj we turned to the southwest. I knew the way because I used to bike there as a child and I'd visited several times in recent years.

The road we traveled from the town of Stryj was relatively good. In the section we traveled, the river valley is surrounded by a string of hills. Viktor's car and the weather today are with us.

Over the past week I'd traveled several times in a car hired by a TV crew that accompanied us. They were filming a documentary to let people know about the dedication of the new wall around the old Jewish cemetery at Bolechów and the root-finding campaign that we have organized.

The driver drove very quickly then, spurred by the TV crew. And here was Viktor, my almost champion of excessively slow driving. When I asked him why he was driving so slowly Viktor said, "You probably noticed the cars following us are not the kind of Lada cars like the one we are traveling in. These new cars are expensive, meaning that their owners are rich and can pay the fine if the cops stop them. I don't have the means to play this game and this car cannot go much faster anyway."

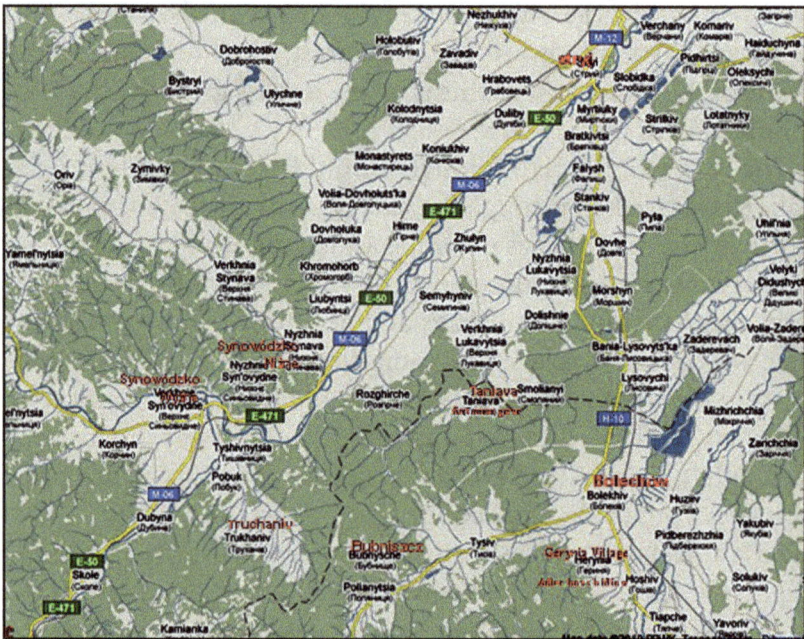

Map of the area and the Stryj River

On the way we pass different villages surrounded by many trees. They are apple trees for the most part. Residents try to sell their fruit. They stand in front of their houses with buckets and baskets full of ripe fruit. The dark blue plums called *Wengerki*, are seen everywhere as an invitation to taste them. Much fruit is lying on the ground and will be used to feed the pigs.

People just seem to slow down. Most of the villagers are busy in the fields. The last weeks of summer are left to harvest the oats and for the last time to hoe the potatoes before collecting them. Many plots of land are yellow after the harvest. But many are still green even though the year was not a particularly rainy one.

We were surrounded by the slopes of the Carpathian Mountains. On the far horizon we saw the tops of the mountains proudly towering high in the direction of the town of Ławoczne on the former border of Hungary.

The Stryj River valley of southeastern Galicia could have been one of the quietest and most pastoral areas. This quietness was, for many years, disturbed by Tatars who came here, Turks and the Cossacks of Khmelnytskyi, and the many wars struck the region in the past. The Austro-Hungarian armies in World War I. The Hungarian and Slovak military moved in this valley during World War II. But between the wars and the savage attacks of the tribes, the area was quiet and pleasant to live in.

Pleasant temperatures at the foot of the Carpathian Mountains attracted travelers and vacationers alike. Several miles to the south they grow grape vines. The region is called the wine country.

Today, the quietness is violated by private cars and many trucks carrying goods across Ukraine or bringing goods from abroad, leading luxury tourist buses and groups of cyclists and riders along the valley. Everyone is travelling on this road leading across the Carpathian Mountains to the former Czech Republic and Hungary to the district of Oblast Zakarpattia which belongs to independent Ukraine nowadays and from there to Hungary and so on.

The railroad tracks run parallel to the road. This route leads from Lwów through the town of Stryj bearing the name of the river toward Ławoczne and Budapest. The name of the Stryj River, according to a legend in old Sikh language "Str" means fast. Nobody knows for sure, if the Stryj River got its name from the city Stryj or vice versa.

Railway stop in the village of Synowódzko Niżne

The river starts to flow in the eastern Beskid Mountains, near the village of Matkiv and Mohnate in the Carpathian Mountains at an altitude of about 1100 meters around the place named Garbek or the big Jawornik. The river flows in a narrow channel that has found its way to crevices while it erodes the ground and the vegetation it meets on its way. Near the town of Turka the river widens and flows in a relatively open area for about 250 kilometers until it meets the Dniester River. Often, in August, the broad bed of the river floods, But today there isn't too much water.

Beyond, the village's right and left riverbanks are overlooked by the slopes of the Carpathian Mountains covered in forests. Apart from a narrow strip of blue water, yellow and green dominate the wide riverbed. We pass the village of Duliby followed by the villages of Koniuchów and Hirne.

Later on I will write about Lubience village. At this point we were approaching the village of Kołyba (a road inn) of which I will also write later. At this place the railway tracks pass under the road and continue to the left, parallel and closer to the river bed.

Before entering the village, the riverbed bends to the left

getting further away from the road and the village. The rail tracks also run slightly away from the road. In this village, nested in a bend of the Stryj River, an Austrian named Gartenberg bought land long ago. On the land he established a successful farm. He had his house built there as well as farm buildings adjacent to this road. It was the last farmhouse in the village. All the land around the house and in the valley, on both sides of the railroad tracks up to the river, belonged to him. This property skirted the village of Międzybrody to the west and that of Baransky's to the east.

To the northwest of the village unrolled the woods of Naked Hip (Hoły Werch) and Kiczer. To the southeast the forests of Tyszowwnica, Truchanow and Bubniszcze could be seen as far as the Sukiel River beyond the hills. The villages of Taniava and Bubniszcze are located in the mountains and forests of the eastern side of the river.

This last village in the mountain features many caves where, according to legend, the robber Dobosz had his headquarters. The caves are located in a deep crevice. Their bottoms are covered in white sand.

According to a legend, one of the wealthiest men in the area was named Potocki. He went to fight Dobosz, the robber, near the village of Synowódzko, and wounded him. The rocks got their color from Dobosz's blood and are still red today. Bubniszcze is probably one of the seven places worthy of interest in Ukraine.

The train station of Synowódzko Niżne was called Synowódzko Bubniszcze before the war because Synowódzko was the nearest train station to Bubniszcze.

The Austrian Gartenberg, gave the farm management to an Orthodox Jew, Baruch Pikholtz as Gartenberg himself lived in Vienna. Baruch was Donia's grandfather.

In 1923 Baruch Pikholtz became the grandfather of a little girl named Dina. My travel was not to follow legends nor the beautiful landscapes that I was accustomed to in my childhood. Even the color of the rocks on the banks of the river Stryj were of no interest to me though they are worth being described. I had a task and therefore will not dwell on such details.

In 2009 I went to this village named Synowódzko Niżne with my son and Viktor who married the granddaughter of the rescuers who were declared Righteous Among the Nations. I wanted to document the unusual rescue of a Jewish couple who were originally from Bolechów - my own town- by a young girl pretending to be a non-Jew named Donia. Viktor had a car and was willing to take me, along with my son David, to visit these places.

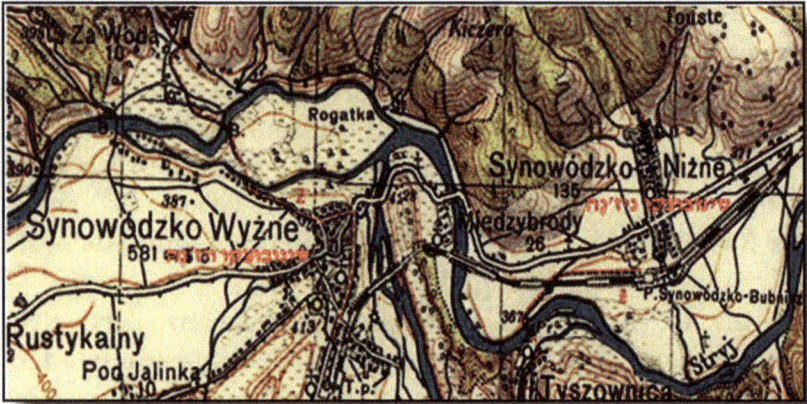

A topographical map of the area of the two villages

I remembered the description of the area and the region as Donia described them to me before I left my home in Israel. I also carefully checked the maps and decided to trust my memory on this matter.

As the car entered the village I discovered things Donia didn't tell me. The maps from before the war didn't describe the changes I ran into. To a senior tourist like me these changes were of interest.

The prewar maps showed a concentration of village houses with a road passing through them. On the east the houses almost touched the railroad tracks and the station. On the west the houses are almost touching the hills. I knew there was a narrow road leading from the main road to the train station. Beyond this road and next to it there was a cluster of houses. The last house on the left was Baruch Pikholtz's house.

Now I discovered that next to every other house there was a

narrow road leading to the railway tracks. But which was leading to the railway station? Having no other choice we stopped. We asked one villager which of these roads was the main one leading directly to Synowódzko-Bubniszcze station.

The man told us where to turn. This unpaved country road had many potholes but it did lead to the station.

Viktor's car started having problems.

"What is happening?" I asked Viktor.

"Nothing special," he replied. "I know what is going on. Once we stop I'll handle it."

We were approaching the place where the road crossed the railroad tracks. The crossing is equipped with an intersection sign, a traffic light and a warning bell.

On our left we saw an empty space that was not too large. At the end we found the railway station building with a sign Synowódzkoovidno Nyżne. The name of Bubniszcze was not mentioned.

At that empty space Viktor stopped the car, lifted the hood and opened the boot. He brought out a manual bicycle pump. He disconnected the gas line to the carburetor. My son David inflated air in this tube and into the tube leading from the gas pump toward the gas tank. The repair was accomplished correctly and the technical experience I gladly wanted to offer was not required.

While they handled the car I approached the train station, a structure of three walls and a roof. It was a kind of a shed that protected travelers from the rain.

A woman approached, seemingly out of nowhere. She was not old enough to explain to us why the station no longer served Bubniszcze village beyond the ridge and the river. She also could not remember the name Pikholtz. This woman realized that the train station once stood on the right side of the road. And the small building across the railroad tracks, according to her, was used in the old days by the guard Pulsa as a house. This corroborated Donia's story.

Another woman, even younger than the first, joined us and she said she had been a teacher there. She had written a book about the area and thought she could be of some help.

When I told her I was from Israel and that I was looking for older people who could show me exactly where the farm manager Mr. Pikholtz once lived, I saw on the face of both of them that they had never heard this name. I told the two women about the Austrian Gartenberg, a wealthy landowner and his mansion in the village whose farm was run by a Jew named Baruch Pikholtz. I also added that these were the last houses of the village. It was about 500 meters from the road leading to the railway station near the main road in the direction of the town of Skole.

The women talked between themselves and came up with the idea that I should meet an older man. They thought he would remember things from the past.

The younger woman was hurrying to her duties but decided to take us to the house of the old man. She led the way. We slowly followed.

After passing a number of houses beyond the train station toward the main road, she turned to the left of the road. Beyond the gate of a typical country house an old couple was standing watching the road.

There was a reason: it's not every day a car passed this way. Many motorcycles yes. But a car?

This intrigued Sanko and his wife. They were wondering why a car would pass by and stop in front of the gate of their house. The young woman explained that I was looking for information about the village and its inhabitants before the last world war. The elderly couple opened the gate after chaining up a loudly barking dog.

Dogs in Ukraine, as anywhere in the world, don't like strangers, especially those who have a cane and invade their kingdom.

I came closer and introduced myself as a native of the nearby town of Bolechów who had come to gather information on the farm owned by Gartenberg and his manager Mr. Pikholtz.

Sanko Taras, the older man, shook my outstretched hand. In the background I heard the young woman who brought us here asked Viktor, "Who is he?" Viktor told her what I had just said in

30

my bad Ukrainian that very moment. "He was born in Bolechów. He is documenting the story of your village in order to write a book."

The couple showed me to a bench in the shade. The man sat down next to me. Taras Ivanovicz began to tell me that in the past he was a train driver in the area. He remembered the conductor Mr. Pulsa and his daughter Viśka. "She came here a few years ago from Poland. Pulsa was a wonderful man." He repeated that several times. Taras Ivanovicz said, "No matter what nation a person belongs to he is good as long as he has a soul and a heart given to him by G_d. Pulsa had a soul and a heart."

I asked him if he remembered the Austrian farm owner Gartenberg. Taras' wife stood next to us. She shook her head like one who can remember but is not sure, or is afraid to tell.

Suddenly Taras recalled the name of Pikholtz. He explaining to his wife, "These are the Pikholtzes that disappeared from the area before the big storm started."

Taras surely remembered how neighbors and friends of his murdered the three Jewish families who lived in the village. They used axes. Not even one German attended these slaughters. He remembered. The Pikholtzes were not among the families who were slaughtered. If the Pikholtzes disappeared from the area, it was before the big storm started.

"Pikholtz was the owner of the farm," said Taras emphatically.

I explained to Taras that Pikholtz was not the owner of the farm. He was just the manager. In 1939 the entire family moved to Stryj. They feared the local Communists who, for many years, had seen them in the area and on the farm. They might have thought as you did and were fearful. They were afraid they might be reported to the Soviets. The Soviets, instead of looking for the farm owner Gartenberg, who lived in Vienna and was out of reach, Pilholtz might be blamed for being the farm's owners and sent to the polar bears; Siberia.

Taras passionately replied, "You are wrong sir. Pikholtz was the farm owner. I even remember the other landowners in the area. Baroński and one of his estates were in the Carpathian Mountains called Gredli. The Gredli brothers converted. The emperor gave them a knighthood before the First World War. Those brothers had agricultural farms at the foot of the Carpathian Mountains. They had a huge wood mill in a place called Krechowice in the area of Dolina and Kalusz. This wood mill had a railway and a private railway station. They all received the land as the Austro-Hungarian Empire was falling apart," Taras Ivanovicz explained.

He continued, "In the twenties, we fought against the Poles. But we were only seven million when they were 30 million. Of course they won and the government here was passed on to the Poles.

(It was Petliura who promised the Ukrainians independence but himself merged with the Poles.) "In those times the Bolsheviks were afraid to enter the area for fear of being beaten by the Poles and the Swedes." (I did not know how Taras could mix up the Swedes from the past centuries with the 20th century).

"You see Mr. Sanko," I said, "The Pikholtz family feared failing memories like yours. You were a young boy then. But people who are your age now could easily be mistaken as you are wrong today. Actually it would have been better for them to have been sent to Siberia. In Siberia they would have had 70% chance of survival. Here they could not survive six months and you know it!"

What he told his wife was burning in my heart, that the Pikholtz family disappeared from the area before the big storm started.

What did he mean by uttering such a statement? What did he call the massacre of the Jews in the villages? A big storm.

I didn't understand the meaning of this phrase. At that point I was boiling. I spoke passionately. For a moment I forgot myself. Why did I come here? I saw a Ukrainian affiliated to the Nationalist group and felt I had to deal with him.

Suddenly I started to cough. I have suffered from asthma for several years and the illness was catching up with me..

Taras noticed that I was hoarse and coughing. "Are you sick?" (Fear of swine flu was running in the Carpathian slopes), and immediately he volunteered a remedy. "You have to prevent your throat from becoming dry,"

I replied, "Of course, I have to use vodka."

"*Karpatska*," the man said. "Vodka? Vodka is not a cure. Certainly you must not drink this poison. It is only a fool's drink."

In the old days *Vodka Wyborowa* was produced. The Poles provided it to people.

Here, again, Taras started blaming the Poles and their leader Pilsudski.

I came to the village to get information and take pictures of the place where the Pikholtz family lived and instead I got a lesson in the history of Ukrainian nationalism. I listened politely but impatiently to Taras' explanation.

To return to our purpose, I told him who I was, where I lived and about the aim of my visit.

After Taras understood, he started to explain his thoughts as to what caused the population to hate the Jews. He said: "When the Austro-Hungarian Empire dissolved, the Cossaks came here as did the Bolcheviks and the Reds of Budiony. The Jews helped Pilsudski and Rydz Smigly dominate the region. Together they abused and starved the Ukrainian population. But Pilsudski was the worst offender. We walked around hungry, wearing torn clothes and they ruled us."

Taras again ignored the fact that the agreements with Pilsudski caused the admiration of the Ukrainians. It was the oppressor Petliura who performed one of the big pogroms against the Jews. It was not the Jews who were guilty of the atrocities.

Taras' arguments reminded me of a Lwów university student who served as a translator for the German TV crew that escorted my international group on our first trip to the area in1996. The head of the TV staff asked her, "What can you say after being with us and this group of Jews for four days after seeing them praying and crying at the mass graves?"

She replied, "Everybody knew the Jews were rich."

At that time I didn't want to make an issue of this reply. Later I asked the head of the TV crew if she thought the Germans thought the same and that's why the Jews had to be annihilated. I suggested that whoever thought this way should read the book by Kazimiera Alberti, *The Cursed Ghetto* written in the early 30s.

I came to this village in order to get information, I could not detain Vikor the entire day and I was not sure I would find someone else in the village older than Taras who had information. I realized that he and his wife knew what I wanted to find out.

I didn't want to get into an argument with him. But I couldn't help saying to him, "Look Mr. Taras Ivanovicz, in this area prior to World War II, most of the population was Ukrainian. The Germans alone couldn't carry out the killings. Do you know, for example, how many Jews survived in Stryj out of about fifteen thousand people? Or in Bolechów and the immediate area, how many survived of about seven thousand."

Taras' answers were in disbelief, "But the Ukrainians never helped the Germans. The Metropolit, like Archbishop Andrei Sheptyts'ky, he saved a lot of Jews. Why wasn't he recognized as a Righteous Gentile?"

Reluctantly I explained to Taras, "There was an argument in the committee that determines the criteria for the degree when it came to the Metropolitan Sheptyts'ky's title Righteous Among the Nations. To my knowledge, the majority of the committee decided not to attribute the Metropolitan Sheptyts'ky the title of Righteous, as the Metropolit was the spiritual father of the SS Wafen Haliczyna infamous, among other crimes, they killed a lot of Jews."

"No way," Taras snapped back. Wafen SS Haliczyna didn't harm the Jews. The Germans killed the Jews. On one Sunday in 1943 at 15.00 the Gestapo accompanied by German foresters and train supervisors of the Gestapo came from Lwów. They rounded up all the Jews from the nearby villages and killed them."

Again Taras was ignoring a sad fact. The Germans, in order not to waste their precious time in handling the Jews, gave a free hand to the Ukrainians living in villages who murdered all using their axes without any German help. I restrained myself with all my strength, trying not to get into an argument with him. I tried to remain impassive. He had seen with his own eyes how his older friends murdered their neighbors.

Boiling, I asked, "And where are all the Jews from the area who were murdered by the Germans buried?"

The young woman replied, "In the forest near Kołyba, right next to the road. I know that Grandma and Grandpa told me they were almost killed there together with the Jews."

"The UPA units (Ukrainian Insurgent Army) and the OUN (Organization of Ukrainian Nationalist) didn't kill Jews either?" I asked.

"They killed only Communists and those who helped Pilsudski," Taras repeated again and again.

I thought to myself, the poor villagers who were helping Marshal Pilsudski. I didn't want to mention to Taras that Ukrainians in the region saw a Communist in every Jew and therefore killed them all.

Wanting to bring Taras to a kind of confession I said, "Can you tell me please why in your opinion a man, no more young, with a sound mind, who has the experience of life, showing love towards other people, would come and visit the area where Jews were killed? This you should have asked the Ribbentrop, Hitler, Himmler and Keitel. Yes sir, you should have asked. I think that Hitler wanted to compete with Stalin. He wanted to kill not only the Jews but to conquer the world. I can even tell you more over, he would have succeeded if the USA and the UK had not joined to fight them."

I could have talked much more to this man. He was too young and probably didn't take an active part in killing Jews. Perhaps, like many others, he had been an informer of Jews in the neighborhood. But only four Jewish families were living in the village and one family had already left in 1939. I had no doubt that Taras was an extreme nationalist and a patriot as were most people in the region.

"Where was the home of Pikholtz?" I asked.

"Was it in the Burke (Burak) Hill?" he questioned.

Burke? I was surprised. Burak means beets in Polish. The man was explaining that the hill bore the name Burke.

"Please could you come with us and show us around?" I asked.

"Sir, I am disabled and barely moving," he replied. "I'll explain to you and the young lady will take you there."

The man began to explain to me and the woman. The words *Burakowa Hirka* (Burak Hill) was mentioned several times. I realized that the place was named after someone called Burak who once lived there and ran away before the return of the Soviets. Probably one of the thirty six Righteous. This is an old Jewish legend about 36 brave men to whom we owe the existence of the world. Awareness and fear of the Red Army did not allow Burak to remain there. I didn't have time to explore the story of Burak.

Every elderly person will agree to talk. At some point they will tell about the wrongdoing without intentionally meaning it.

Taras explained to the woman how to travel a particular way to the left, where the end of the village once stood. Across this way, that was the area of Burak. I realized that almost every word fit Donia's story.

When I was there I didn't realize that the place was named after Donia's grandfather Baruch who the Jews of the village called Burech. The locals heard Burke or Burak. It became clear to me when I went back home and Donia found the connection.

The woman, our guide, was very busy. But I explained to her that I needed information to write a story about this particular village and she agreed to guide us for the next half hour

Taras said goodbye. I give him a bill of $5 for the time he had spent with me. Taras turned the bill for all parties to see.

"What is this? Are these dollars?" Taras asked in a tone like someone who had never seen an American dollar before.

"Yes," I said leaving Sanko's place.

"Very good. It will allow me to celebrate. Tomorrow is Ukraine Independence Day," he answered.

We got back into the car and, over the way full of bumps and potholes, we went back to the main road in the center of the village, turned left toward the southwest in the direction of the town of Skole. Later, after about a 500 meter drive through the village, the woman told Viktor to turn left and drive to a narrow alley and stop.

On the way the young woman explained, pointing in the opposite direction we were heading, "There, in Cołyba, at the mass grave area, large and beautiful cherry trees are growing. My grandmother forbade me to pick the cherries saying, "Don't pick cherries. They are growing on the blood of the Jews."

The woman's face was sad. I don't know if it was genuine sadness that her grandfather was almost killed together with the Jews or because of the mass grave full of innocent people whose only crime was to have been Jewish. Those were people whom they heard about but did not know.

The story contradicts everything that was written about the murder of the Jews of these villages.

During my visit to Ukraine so far I'd only met genuine sadness from the family of the Righteous who saved me and my cousin. Faces looked sad when they talk about the past they heard about from their parents and grandparents. Perhaps the new *Bon Ton* (sophisticated upper class) in Ukraine is to show sympathy. Maybe it is one of the first harbingers of a new spring.

"You are the first Jews I've ever met," said the young woman.

When we got out of the car the woman pointed to the first house on the right corner of the alley and said, "Here once stood the house where the Pikholtz family lived. This whole area Synowódzko Niżne, on this spot, the Pikholtz house once stood is called Burak Hill. All the plots on which the houses now stand were distributed by the Soviet authorities in the early fifties."

An older woman joined us. She was new to this area and could not answer the questions relating to the past. She arrived here in the 50s so, of course, she didn't remember the Pickholtz family or even the house where they lived that is now gone into oblivion.

"Around here there is not even one building built before World War II," said the older woman."

The young one agreed with her.

Synowódzko Niżne:
On this spot the Pikholtz house once stood

I was at a loss. What will I show Donia when I return? Then I turned to the young woman and asked her what she would do in my place.

The woman suggested we continue down the narrow road toward the river by saying one word, "*Landschaft*."

I did not expect to hear this word spoken so naturally after 90 years or more since the Austrians ruled this area. The landscape. Why didn't I think of that?

"Sir," the young woman disturbed my thoughts. "The *landschaft* has not changed in thousands of years. The girl running to the train station to go to school in Stryj must have used this path."

I agreed with the woman immediately. Without a doubt Donia will recognize the view.

"The whole area was empty of houses from the old days. You show her the *landshaft* and topographical structure of the area and she will immediately recognize her birthplace."

Synowódzko Niżne: The narrow road
swerved suddenly to the right

Thus spoke the young woman while walking down the alley while Viktor followed with the car. After about 150 meters, the narrow road swerved suddenly to the right. Ahead was a steep slope of Synowódzko Niżne: the narrow road swerved suddenly to the right about two or three meters. The area then became significantly lower. It continued gradually to the riverbed. Down close to the slope there were rows of houses with gardens and orchards.

To the left, toward the train station, there was a pedestrian path which most probably Donia used day after day to and from the station. Or perhaps she walked across the empty fields until she reached the station.

We made a right turn down from Burak Hill and arrived at the open field. We kept going to a junction where a pretty narrow path led down to the Burak Hill side while the other path slightly turned to the left as if toward the river.

We chose the left road, went another 50 meters and stood in the middle of a hayfield. On our right and in front of us we saw rows of corn. At a distance of about 200 meters we saw the railroad tracks. Beyond the tracks, just about another 300 meters, we could see the mountain slopes, along the eastern Stryj riverbed.

I was happy this was the way Donia took to have a swim with her friends. Here, at the foot of Burak Hill, she picked wildflowers and berries. I could picture the girls and boys.

Synowódzko Niżne: "Burak" Hill
as seen from the East

The voice of the young woman interrupted my thoughts. She suggested that I take pictures of the area. "Here, to the right of Burak Hill (*Burakowa Hirka*) we just went down, move left along the hill, southwest then south and around. Take the entire valley and surrounding ridges. No doubt the girl is still fond of the memories of these landscapes and will recognize them immediately," she said.

My son David started filming the whole panorama just as the woman suggested. First he filmed the way we just came down from Burak Hill toward the valley. It was easy to see the number of houses alongside the small slope and the road that went down from the west. Then he filmed along Burak Hill. The camera moved to the hill near the main road where Donia's house once stood. David kept photographing along the hill, southwest, then south and around. He took film of the entire valley and the surrounding ridges.

"There is no doubt that the girl has engraved in her memory these landscapes and will recognize them immediately."

Now the camera travelled from the mountains to the valley from the southwest meeting again at the railroad tracks.

"In the hills across the river, do you see a huge single rock?" the woman asked. "Around this rock excavations were carried out. In the past a well-known Ukrainian writer Ivan Franko visited this place. The place is called Horodyszcze."

Now, in August 2009, we had the privilege of photographing this remote place.

Childhood in the Village of a Hostile Population

Donia lost track of time. Her mind was fuzzy. She saw herself as a little girl in Synowódzko Niżne village at the foot of the Carpathian Mountains and the wonderful forests around there.

The spring of 1939 was approaching. And the *kosher* pure stone ground wheat flour was prepared by the family. This flour was for homemade *matzo*. Everything must be strictly *kosher*, prepared meticulously and extremely pure. A batch of *matzo* was sent every year to Yitzhak Moshe Raitenberg, the Rabbi of Skole. *Kosher* cheese, prepared at home, was sent to the Rabbi for the holiday of *Shavuot*. Beeswax candles, home-made by grandmother Yocheved, were send to the *Rebbe* (as he was called) for *Rosh Hashanah*.

Donia loved the preparation for the holidays. Now the preparations were for *Passover*. The great stove, where the weekly bread and *bulbovnik* (a potato delicacy), was baked, swept and thoroughly washed. No crumb of *chumetz*: bread, cake or baked goods from the past year could be left.

The stove was cleaned and then heated with a lot of wood. Next to the stove I imagine the women. Donia was among them.

They were rolling flat the pieces of dough. Then Grandfather Baruch put them on a long wooden paddle and quickly stuck the paddle into the oven. He placed it on the hot surface of the oven floor.

As he rolled the dough for a second time he took the baked *matzos* (unleavened bread) out of the oven. Grandpa had to hurry so the *matzo* didn't burn. Toward the end of the day a pile of freshly prepared *Passover matzo* was placed in huge baskets lined with white tea cloths.

Donia loved watching all the activity at home. She was intrigued to know how Grandma's maid Nastunia started the fire under the kitchen stove. Nastunia first opened a small iron door at the bottom of the stove. This door had a small opening that allowed one to check if the fire was burning properly. Inside you could see an opening that had a steel frame with steel bars. Using a long hook, Nastunia lifted the frame and took it out. Then she removed the pieces of wood or coal left behind from the previous cooking or baking.

In the lower part of the stove next to the floor, there was a smaller iron door which Nastunia opened and, with the same hook, she took out all the ashes with a dustpan. "What do you do with the ashes?" Donia asked.

"Look my girl," said Nastunia. "Some of the residue still contains big pieces of coal and wood. I'll use them again as burning material. The smaller pieces of coal I throw away. The ash dust will be used to clean and polish silver or to add to the soap in order to get very white laundry."

Then, the maid opened the larger door again. Nastunia replaced the frame with its thick iron bars. The frame was arranged in dense rows of bars with small intervals between them.

"Why are there bars?" asked Donia.

"Soon you will see how I light the wood and you will understand for yourself why these bars are used," replied the maid.

Nastunia came close to the wall. She pulled out a small handle saying, "This is a chimney regulator, a flue. It allows the smoke to leave and ventilates the fire."

"In winter, after cooking and baking, you have to slightly close the flue to keep the residual heat in the house and not allow it to go up the chimney."

The maid put wrinkled newspaper on top of the bars and over the paper she put thin wood chips. Then she took a box of matches out of her pocket and set fire to the paper. It didn't take long for the chips to catch on fire. Now the maid began to lay down some thicker pieces of wood, then some even larger ones.

"Oak is hard wood and burns for a long time," she explained to Donia, closing the lower door of the oven but not before Donia had time to see how sparks and ash fell down through the iron bars.

Now Nastunia moved the latch on the bottom door and reduced the gaps to the minimum required airflow.

Donia was not only interested in the oven or the stove. She loved to sit and watch how her mother prepared dough for *challah* (*Shabbat* bread). It was wonderful.

On the kitchen table her mother put a big wooden board called *lokszen breith* (a noodle board). Her mother put a large flat gridded sieve on the board. From a large bag, with the help of a scoop, her mother took flour and poured it into the sieve. Then her mother began to shake the sieve right and left. The sifted flour fell onto the noodle board. Donia's mother threw the leftover flour in the sieve to the chickens in the yard. She put the sifted flour into a large bowl, made a hole in its center and put yeast and a sour smelling mixture into it. Mother covered the bowl with a large towel and went to attend to other chores.

Donia asked her mother to call her when she was ready to work with the dough. An hour later, her mother called Donia. The dough mixture was ready for the next step. Mother added water to the flour and began to mix until dough was formed. When the dough was ready mother spread some flour over it. Once again she covered the bowl with a towel and placed the bowl not far from the stove so that the dough could receive its warmth. The warmth caused it to rise.

Donia's mother returned to her other chores and Donia went

into the garden. After about two hours Donia's mother called her. She wanted to show her the rest of the bread making procedure. When Donia entered the kitchen, her mother picked up the towel covering the bowl and Donia could see how much the dough had risen. The bowl was overflowing.

Donia's mother generously sprinkled some flour onto the noodle board and then transferred the dough onto the board. She began kneading the dough until it became supple and elastic. Donia was allowed to stick her finger into the dough. She watched the holes she created fill back up.

When the kneading was done and the dough was smooth and ready, Donia's mother split it into equal sized balls. Then she started kneading them again, each one separately. And then she let each rise under a towel for an extra half hour. She made long round sausage shapes with the dough and hung them over a string, making them click together. With the help of a knife she cut the end of each, stitching them together. Donia's mother would then start braiding the sausages of dough as though they were a girl's hair. Mother made two other *challahs* this way. The finished pieces of art she would put in a mold greased with oil. The *challah* was brushed with egg wash and put into the oven after about an hour. Donia could see the magic of *challah* baking. It was for a special dinner for *Shabbat* (Sabbath) on Friday evening.

First mother would light the candles. Two loaves of *challah* were covered with an embroidered tea cloth. Then, after Dad returned from praying, he washed his hands and then cut one of the *challah* into small pieces. He dipped his piece into salt and made a blessing. Thank G_d for having bread from the land. Then the family gathered around the table.

Donia was also interested in noodle making. The noodle board was used once again. The dough was left to rise for some time in a bowl and then transferred to the noodle board. Much more flour was added to allow the dough to dry until it became very dry. Then her mother would divide the dough according to what she wanted to use it for: some became noodles, some became flakes or crumbs. Then Donia's mother hand rolled the dough on the board until it was shaped like a ball. A rolling pin was used to flatten each ball into a big round, thin sheet. Mother would fold the sheet several times and, with a sharp knife, cut it into narrow pieces.

From time to time Donia's mother would stop cutting the noodles and push them aside. She would add a little more flour to keep them from sticking. It went this way until Donia's mother reached the amount of noodles she thought she needed to feed her family. Whatever she didn't need became flakes or crumbs. Donia's interest was an anticipation of the future.

When the holidays came closer the activity was more intense at home. The maid was busy polishing the whole house, inside and out. Family members helped her and the house was cleaned from top to bottom.

Over the holidays Donia's aunt from Ławoczne came with her daughters and stayed with them. It was fun as her cousins were the same age.

Grandfather ran the farm but always found free time to show his grandchildren how to grow vegetables in the small patches they had been allotted.

Everyone learned to recognize and to get rid of the weeds that constantly grew. Little patches of land had been granted for the training of the younger generation. Each child received seeds from their grandfather and the summer holidays could attest to their efforts.

The farm was immense. The land expanded on both sides of the railroad tracks and as far as the river on the east. Occasionally Grandpa would go to the village of Lubieńce where the Regional Head Office was located. It represented the interest of the rich Mr. Gartenberg.

Grandpa also liked to visit Isaiah Diamand in his home or at his inn. Isaiah, an Orthodox Jew, had a tiny farm. When, in Isaiah's opinion, the land did not provide enough return to sustain a large family, he opened a pub near the main road between the town of Stryj and Skole where travelers could get food and drinks or simply meet one another.

In addition to the pub Isaiah Diamand provided milk to the Jewish community of Stryj and was even a cattle dealer in

Vienna. One of Isaiah's son immigrated to Canada where he became very wealthy. The two friends would sit in the bar and discuss their situation and the news. Isaiah complained that his business in Vienna stopped as the Nazis forbade buying cattle if Jewish hands were in the deal. Isaiah once said he heard a rumor that the Nazis forbade management jobs to Jews. "The bastards evoke the waves of anti-Semitism here. Who knows how long it will take Gartenberg to stop paying me a salary?"

Once Grandpa brought news from Lubieńce: the Metropolit Andrei Sheptyts'kyi, the spiritual leader of the Ukrainians, would come visiting their village in the spring. When the Metropolit came he should be received with all the pomp due his rank. On that day the bells of the churches must ring loudly. The adults in the family must wear their Sunday clothes. Grandfather and Donia's father stood in front of the house holding the *Torah* scrolls, a sign of high respect to the personality passing in front of the house.

Donia had just finished the fourth grade and the summer vacation had started. She was spending time with her cousin Chaja and Chaja's sister, younger by a year and a half. They joined the rest of the cousins who came to visit grandfather over the summer holidays.

They all stayed outside where Donia played with her sisters. They were full of enthusiasm. They played with the children who were riding far away to the place where bigger carts were bringing in the grain. The girls went to watch the milking of the cows and berry picking on a nearby hill. Religious girls were not allowed to be away from their homes. They couldn't go beyond the hill where they picked wild strawberries and raspberries that grew in abundance.

This could be done in a village on the beautiful summer days. Who needs to visit nearby towns or villages?

The River Stryj flows not far from the village. It is a mountainous river. Its current is strong but it slackens its strength and there are places where you can swim or just dip as in the *Mikvah* (the ritual bath). The river banks are covered in thick bushes. Girls could swim there and nowhere else.

On the way home, walking across meadows, they pick flowers and braided wreaths made from these wild flowers. Life was fine. One just has to be careful not to run into anti-Semites or drunks. Jewish boys, adults and courageous people walked and climbed up Parshko, the highest mountain or crossed the Stryj River, or walked along paths up to a beautiful place in the Carpathian Mountains: the caves of robber Dobosz in Bubniszcze. When they got back they told about their impressions and adventures to children who are enthralled with their tales.

Backpackers from all over Poland occasionally passed through the village. They wanted to enjoy the beauty of the green mountains and the diffusion of the resin scent of the pine trees that grow on the slopes.

The village was not short of hooligans and anti-Semites, even at school. Once in a while these children shouted, "You pariah Jew." The Ukrainian teacher defended both Jewish students, saying it is not nice to talk like that. Once, the entire family was threatened.

This is what Donia said. She was about ten at the time.

One night her Grandfather announced that the cow was about to give birth. Donia wanted to see the birth; the miracle of nature. They went to the barn with a kerosene lamp. The little girl noticed a letter stuck on the barn door.

"Look grandpa, someone left a letter for us." It was written in Ukrainian and terrible. "If the Pikholtzes don't give $ 1,000 to those who left the letter, we will do the same to them that we did to that family in the Kalna village."

Donia asked grandpa for an explanation. Baruch told her, "In the village of Kalna thugs and criminals wanted to extort money from a Jewish family who lived there. The family had a small grocery store and their income didn't allow them to pay the ransom or they didn't want to pay such an amount. The result was the killing of seven members of their family. The murderers threw their bodies into a large box where flour was stored.

In order not to upset them, he forbade Donia from telling the rest of the family. Donia became the messenger and brought the letters between the grandfather and the criminals.

In another letter it was stipulated that if the police were notified, everyone would be killed.

After some time, it was explained in one letter where to put the money. Grandpa paid $500 so that the family continued to live in safety.

Donia's brother Yitzhakl, the youngest in the family, was born in 1927. He went for a swim in the river with the Rebbe and his school friends. They went to a difference place than the girls.

The Stryj River and its tributaries provide abundant fish. On Fridays the traditional carp or pike were served. On holidays a tasty trout was served.

The Pikholtz children did not only play games during the summer vacation. They had to take care of their own garden as well. It was a challenge between them as to who grew the best vegetables. Grandfather Baruch controlled how the children handled their private patch; how to weed; how to use fertilizer; how vegetables were grown. He expressed his opinion on the results. He used to say, "Yitzhakl, you are the smallest. You must learn from your sisters. See how they weed the carrots, radishes or other vegetables. See what they do. How they remove the weeds. This must be done or the weeds will suck the nutrients from the earth and no vegetables will grow."

"Gitale, your flower bed looks good. But if you gave it a bit more compost, it would look better."

Grandpa didn't know that Gitale had no interest in her garden and even more, she hated dealing with cow dung.

Each child, in turn, received comments and blessings from their grandfather.

The children proudly brought carrots, beetroots, cucumbers and fresh tomatoes to their mother in the kitchen. On the way to the kitchen the grandchildren showed Grandfather Baruch their crops.

At the end of the summer, prior to going back to school, the grandfather would give every child a little prize according to his or her achievement. Donia felt some responsibility toward Gitale who was three years younger. She helped her and guided her to the limit of her abilities.

Libke was two years older than Donia. She behaved well. When she came to the village, Libke stayed with her grandparents, Taube and David Samuel Pikholtz, in Stryj. She was at school at *Beit Jacob* studying bookkeeping. Libke loves to embroider and sew. She even tried to teach Donia the art of embroidery during one of the holidays when she came home.

The village spanned a small tumultuous mountain river full of rocks. Local fishermen were sometimes successful in catching trout in the middle of this river.

The Pikholtz grandfather, Baruch, and Donia's parents lived in two apartments in the very large house on the farm they managed. Their house was about half a mile from the village. It was near the main road that led to Synowódzko Wyżne and the town of Skole. In the village besides themselves, three other Jewish families lived on small pieces of land barely making a living by farming and so they worked in Synowódzko Wyżne at the sawmill. They brought their produce to the market in Stryj.

Donia loved nature. She loved to work in the fields and excelled at what Baruch taught her.

Donia's father made sure all the children knew how to manage money. Everyone had to contribute in one way or another to the family income. Donia knew all that and did her homework. This knowledge would not hurt them if one day, G_d willing, they wanted to go to Palestine. They would not have to go through training. They would be skilled farmers.

Grandfather Baruch was an Orthodox Jew and a farmer. He insisted that, along with the fear of Heaven, observing the rules, studying the *Torah* and daily prayers, he should work and bring the family a decent enough life.

In those days before the Second World War, and even before that in Galicia, there were many Orthodox families working in agriculture. All these plots of land were enough to sustain them. They were satisfied with the fields and serving the Creator. Others, with bigger families, in order to provide a livelihood for their families and educate their children, kept taverns or engaged in commerce.

In this region the Backenroth family were Orthodox Jews

and farmers and had been established here for generations. G_d blessed them and in their arid land a natural treasure was discovered: OIL. Thanks to this treasure, the family received a knighthood.

The names and happiness of the Backenroth was famous all over Poland. Their wealth was so extreme that the father gave a dowry to his daughter: a house and a distillery in Bolechów.

The Jews in the area knew the miracle that happened to the Backenroth family and would say in Yiddish, "*Dos zenen gevirim adirim.*" ("Those are mighty Lords.") Jews prayed to the Lord to make a similar miracle happen to them. There was a rumor that Jewish farmers drilled on their land under the pretext of searching for water in the hope of finding black gold.

Grandfather Baruch had four sons and two daughters. Five of his children were married.

Aunt Macia, Donia's
mother's sister

Aunt Malka Donia's
mother's sister

They were all religious and hard workers. Donia's parents, her mother Shaindel who was one of eleven children and father Matityahu (Mathes) who was one of six children, raised their own children in the spirit of the *Torah* and that of work. Wheat, rye and buckwheat were grown on the farm and animals were raised too. It also had a large orchard.

Aunt Mechla, Donia's mother's sister
and her husband Mechel Koch

Further away, about two kilometers from the house, near
the train tunnel, the Pikholtz family had another house. It had
several rooms that were used by the extra hands employed for
the harvest. These workers came from Smorże, a village in the
Carpathian Mountains, where they themselves owned little
plots of land. The soil on their farms was not fertile enough
and yielded poor crops; not enough to support their families.
Therefore, during the harvest season, these small farmers came
to the Pikholtz's farm to make some cash to help them meet ends
till the next season. These workers settled in this other building,
prepared their own food and what they needed for a month or
two while they stayed there.

The Pikholtz family was well off and gave money secretly to
the poor and booked guests for *Shabbat* and the holidays. Two
large rooms were dedicated to the guests in their home. They
were equipped with comfortable, clean beds and warm linens.
The visitors brought their own clothes.

Grandfather Baruch and Donia's father Matityahu were
followers of the rabbi from Czortków. During the week they
wore hats and grey suits but for *Shabbat* and holidays they wore
black suits and a *shtreimel*. *Shtreimel* is Yiddish, and it refers to a

specific type of fur hat that *Hasidic* Jewish men wear on *Shabbat*, Jewish holidays, and other festivities.

One room in the Pikholtz home had a wall orientated to the East. It was reserved as a synagogue. There the Ark stood holding their private *Torah*.

People in the area spoke of the family's hospitality. Many poor Jews would come to them. And there were many miserable people between the two world wars. Eastern Galicia was considered one of the poorest in the whole Austro Hungarian Empire. The global economic crisis of the late twenties didn't spare this region either.

On cold winter days there were a few guests arriving before the Sabbath. In the summer they would arrive on foot covered in dust. And in the winter they arrived frozen. Beggars could not afford the luxury of even a third class ride on the train. In summer, before they reached the Pikholtz home, they would shake the dust from their clothes and wash in one of the many rivers. In winter, with the assistance of Nastunia, the frozen guests were taken to their room. There they would take off their wet shoes and leggings and put them near a heater to dry.

Then they were given a cup of hot tea in grandmother Yocheved's kitchen to warm themselves. When they were warm enough they began to tell news from "the entire world."

It was wonderful for the guests to reach this family's home as they were provided with good food and comfortable accommodations; things they lacked in their poor homes.

At the Pikholtz home a long weekend was really a pleasure. The house had a *Shtebel* (a chapel) to pray. No need to go further. And the food was good and abundant. The Pikholtzes made their guests understand that they were necessary. If they didn't come there wouldn't be enough men to form a *minyan*, the necessary ten man quorum for the prayers. This way it was a benefit for everyone; the family and the guests. Grandpa Baruch made a point of honor that on Sabbath and holidays they would have guests under their roof.

In previous years the topic for talks with guests ran around the weekly *Torah* section, livelihood issues, success stories and so on, even dreams "Ah! If we were Rothschilds."

In the 30s more and more guests spoke with the Pikholtzes. Even political problems were discussed as were the lack of possibilities to emigrate and the risks incurred by the Jews.

Youth reveals nonsense; finding street posters denouncing the corruption of the government. Red flags were tied to telephone posts, not just on May First. Poles chased young Jews with Communist propaganda and arrested them. Both guests and hosts tried to understand where this was leading. If only these crazy young people used this time to study the *Torah* or attend the synagogue and respect their parents. The government would not have any reason to chase them. What could be done about the incitement of the Ukrainian Nationalists? Even their teenagers fill the cells at Brigitki and Bereza Kartuska prisons. The great majority of them were anti-Semites; Jew haters who longed for an independent Ukraine.

They met young Jews with a leftist approach in the prisons and tried to convert them to a Communist ideal world. But in return the Jewish prisoners were beaten.

Polish student nationalists organizations harassed Jewish students on every campus. Jewish students were severely beaten and often sent to the hospital with broken limbs and knife wounds. They were hostage between the Polish hammer and the Ukrainian anvil. This was the conclusion both hosts and guests reached.

It was not easy to keep a Jewish religious life in Synowódzko Niżne. There were not enough Jewish families to have their own *Shoat* or a real Synagogue. This was why the Pikholtz family created a chapel in their home, a *Shteble*. A *melamed*, (a religious teacher) lived with them year-round teaching little brother Yitzhakl the *Talmud*, *Gemara* and other religious learning. The teacher was with them for years.

Mr Lifshitz, who was from the village of Tyszownica located on the eastern bank of the Stryj River, used to come there to pray on Saturdays and holidays. The Lifshitzes were the only Jewish family to live in this village. They owned the ferry. All coachmen from the Carpathian Mountains villages across the river who carried wood logs to the sawmills of Synowódzko Wyżne were obliged to use this ferry. Mr. Lifshitz would collect a fee from carts and travelers for passing the Stryj River. Mr. Lifshitz always had a lot on his hands. On Saturday and holidays some trusted non-Jew would replace him.

As previously mentioned, there was no *Shochat* or synagogue, in Synowódzko Niżne village. For the ritual slaughtering of chickens, Jews were forced to go to the larger village of Synowódzko Wyżne where a ritual slaughterer lived. The butcher came to their village once every other week to perform the ritual killing.

When Donia started attending school, in order to have *kosher* meat in the house on Saturday, even if the butcher had visited the village on that week, the girl had to take one or two chickens on the train which she would bring home after school. Donia was a bit ashamed in front of her friends who travelled with her. But she did not dare to say NO to her mother.

After arriving in Stryj on her way to school, Donia would stop at her grandma Yocheved's house and leave the chickens. At the end of the school day Donia collected the chickens from Yocheved's and went to the butcher so that he could slaughter them after which she went home by train. This slaughtering made Donia miss the regular train she took with her school friends.

A year later, when the child had grown up a bit, Sheindel realized that Donia was ashamed to travel with the chickens in her school bag. Mother agreed that the week the butcher did not come to the village the girl would bring *kosher* beef from Stryj.

On weekdays and on Saturday the families ate their meals separately. The grandparents did not eat alone as they always had guests.

Donia loved the holiday evenings when they shared meals with guests and her grandparents. There was a lot of preparation around the huge table.

Women, after they returned from *Ezrat Nashim*, (the room adjacent to the men's prayer room) prepared the table, a festive spread for the men to eat after praying. The men were a little late because of a conversation or a political debate that arose with the men from the neighboring villages.

Men accompanied by their guests left the *Shteble*. They would wash their hands and then sit at the big table loaded with holiday dishes and the best possible food. Grandpa would break the *challah*. He would distribute a piece to everyone as they recited a ritual prayer. Everyone said the ritual prayer over the bread but the guests found it necessary to add a special benediction prayer for their hosts thanking them for their hospitality. They also thanked them for the delicacies placed before them on the table.

Taube, Shaindel's mother, Donia, and her sisters served the gefilte fish and all the food. At the end of the meal Nastunia removed the empty dishes and trays.

Everyone celebrated the food and sang *Eshet Chail* (the heroism of the wife). The women went into the kitchen to return the leftovers in the cabinet or the basement and the men would sit in the living room and, as usual, discuss and interpret the *Parsha*, the specific part of the Bible read that the week.

The children of the village attended school in the village of Synowódzko Niżne until fourth grade. After the summer vacation Donia was registered to go to Kingi on Batorego Street in Stryj. To go there Donia would have to ride the train to school and back every day. She couldn't wait for the end of the holidays. She imagined the new school. How would she adapt to it? Who would be her schoolmates? Would all the pupils of her village go to this school?

The summer vacation was finally over. The next day was the big day for Donia. She was so excited she could hardly sleep. When she heard the first call of the rooster, she jumped out of bed, washed herself and dressed in nice clothes. On the first day in her new school she wanted to look nice. She was now a big girl, riding a train to Stryj to attend fifth grade. She was confident she would learn more interesting things than what she learned in the fourth grade in Synowódzko Niżne.

While bundling her new books her parents had purchased for her on the teacher's recommendation, she gave a quick glance at their contents. She noticed how much more difficult they seemed.

The King School was located on the street named for the

famous King Stephan Batory and was a high level school. On her first day in this new school and the trip to Stryj her mother accompanied her. Donia felt that the walk to the train station seemed to take a long time. Heaven forbid she would be late.

After half an hour's boring walk they reached the train station of Synowódzko-Bubniszcze and waited for the train. Donia's friend Hanaleh Hauptman, the only other Jewish pupil who had attended her village school, was already there waiting not far from the railroad tracks. Of the many other non-Jewish pupils, some had been in her class and others were not.

Their village didn't have a real station. The train would stop only two or three minutes, just the amount of time necessary for passengers to get off or board the train. It was not a full station. The passengers bought their tickets directly from the conductor, Pulsa, who was at the same time controlling the validity of tickets purchased in advance and controlled those just sold. He knew all of his passengers. He came up to Donia and her mother, touched his hat with one finger and said, "Good morning ladies. I guess Mrs. Pikholtz we have a new traveler to school? Would you like to purchase a monthly pass? It's cheaper."

Donia blushed and bowed her head. Her mother replied, "Good morning Mr. Pulsa. You haven't visited the farm in a long time. You've stopped coming and enjoying the stuffed cabbage or stuffed fish, *Ryba po Zydowsku*, (Jewish style fish) you like so much."

"How could I forget these delicacies you fed me when I visited your farm? My wife Stefa is not in good health. So I hardly ever leave the house except to go to work. What kind of tickets do you want?"

"Please, Mr. Pulsa, a return ticket from Stryj for me and, for Donia, the monthly special price student pass."

Conductor Pulsa opened a leather bag hanging from his shoulder and took out two cards. He punched each one. Holding out the tickets, he requested the payment. He asked if the child needed to be told how to use the card.

"Thank you Mr. Pulsa. She already knows how to handle it but I will remind her anyway."

56

In those days stories went around about older people who traveled by train carrying bags stuffed with books as if they were going to study somewhere in order to get a discount. We called them students forever. Or in the winter they could carry a pair of mini skis showing in this way that they were sportsmen and for this reason entitled to have a sportsman discount.

When they reached Stryj Donia and her mother walked to the school where she was to be a pupil. On the way they passed her grandparent's house. They lived not far from the school on Lwówska Street number 21. Her grandparents knew it was a big day for their granddaughter and waited outside their house to wish her lots of success with her learning.

From that day on Donia would go on her own to the train station and after a ride of 30 minutes she was in Stryj. Donia usually took a shortcut to the station. She didn't take the road crossing the village but would cut through the farm's orchard and in less than ten minutes she was at the train stop.

The young girl visited her grandparents once in a while but sometimes, when a blizzard was raging, she would stay overnight with them.

Grandpa David Samuel died in 1937 and from that time on Donia visited her grandmother more often and frequently stayed overnight. (Grandma was murdered with the rest of the family in the *Great Aktion*.)

Donia remembers the Polish language teacher Mrs. Wielgożyńska, the math teacher, Mrs. Bielawska and the Ukrainian language teacher, Mrs. Płoszczańska. Donia doesn't remember any extreme anti-Semitism at school. The reason is probably because the Jewish children represented about 50% of the pupils. She remembers a school friend Lola Weiss who also survived the Holocaust.

Sounds of War

"Jews are not showing allegiance. They will not serve in the army should Hitler attack Poland."

These anti-Semitic remarks started to be heard despite the

equal number of students in both communities, Jewish and non-Jewish. This mood started to be felt all over Poland. Anti-Semitism began to raise it head more and more.

Donia would come home and tell her parents what was going on among the pupils at school and what she heard in Stryj.

Taube, her grandmother, was concerned about the possibility the Berlin madman would attack Poland.

"No doubt a war is imminent" the *Shabbat* guests clearly stated. "After all, they had just arrived from town and there it is no secret. Hitler will not abandon the idea of a corridor between the free city of Danzig and East Prussia."

At the train station and the house of the Mayor there was a banner that showed a great number of guns. In the middle there was a representation of the commander in chief of the army, Pilsudski's successor, Marshall Rydz Śmigły. At the bottom of the poster it read, "STRONG, UNITED and READY."

Those who had common sense said, "The tough and stubborn Polish pride will bring a disaster upon us all. Look how this crazy man took over Austria. Big countries like France and Great Britain have already given him Czechoslovakia. Does a similar fate also await Poland?"

Questions of these type were heard from people who knew; the guests who came for *Shabbat* and who would directly tell grandfather Baruch and father Mathes.

Poverty did not stop them from being interested in politics. They did not have to worry about property. They took care of their lives. That was their only property.

"Would these events bring back another world war?"

The question was, would the Jews be able to escape this time? (During World War I, in fear of the Cossacks and the pogroms, the Jews who could afford it ran away and headed to Czechoslovakia.)

Now that Austria didn't exist anymore, the Czech Republic was under the rule of this madman and Hungary recently voiced anti-Semitic stands.

"We are paupers and have no means of escape. We should be careful not to help the locals bring another Petliura. The rich won't have a place to run to and the war will bankrupt them. What will happen to us, the poor?" The poor guests would speak this way.

"We should not alarm the Pikholtz family. We should get out of here or our predictions could come true. We, the poor, will be the spoilage right away, even before the first shot is fired. Where can we find another place like this one? We can come here where we are given food and we can relax."

"Poland is another thing," the insiders would say. "Its allies, France and England, will stop this crazy man and will curb his madness."

The cynics would add, "So the hymn says. Bonaparte gave us an example of how to win."

Despite all the chattering and the opinions expressed by insiders and allies, Poland began to seriously prepare for war - but a bit late.

The defense ministry published a Recruiting Yearbook to enforce compulsory army service. The military doctors were careful to accept everyone: a flat foot not long ago was a reason not to be mobilized. Now such a soldier would not serve in the fields but would be used in an office or as a cook. Reservists who were in need of training and briefing were called to their units. Adult men were called in for anti-air defense training.

Army officials came to villages checking the horses worth recruiting. These were selected and counted and their owners were told that they would be drafted in due course.

The first of September 1939 arrived. The very day Donia had to go back to school in Stryj.

Despite the discordant news of the coming war she had prepared herself to return to school. As in the previous years she got up early, dressed in nice clothes as required of the first day back to school.

Donia arrived where the train stopped. But oh, what a surprise. The long time conductor and director of this stopover in the village Mr. Pulsa said: "Kids! There is no need to go to school in Stryj. The war has started. Go back home."

Pulsa, the good neighbor, was well meaning. He surpassed

the limits of his job by warning the children about going to Stryj. The Polish State Railways (PKP) lost *złotys* provided by the fare of the commuting school children.

Several people came from Stryj and told the villagers that Stryj had just been bombed by German planes. The villagers kept listening to the few radios in the village: at a Ukrainian family's house (He had recently returned from America.); at Mr. Pulsa and the teacher's home as well. Indeed the announcer said that the Germans attacked Poland by surprise. Then there were a number of warnings and alerts about planes coming.

"Uwaga, Uwaga. Nadchodzi, Nadchodzi." "Attention, attention. Approaching, approaching."

Quite often, in a sad and disorderly way, the announcer warned without specifying where the danger zone was. As a result, the people just didn't know exactly what the announcer meant. That was the way the Poles were getting themselves ready to go to war.

Despite all the talk and the requirements of the Germans, the Austrian and Czechoslovakian precedents, the Poles suddenly felt surprised and deceived.

The Poles themselves described such a scenario: "The Germans would invite them to a meeting and when they kissed their hands, as was the ancient Polish custom, they would realize that the Germans were angry and that the war was inevitable."

The bloody Nazis attacked with full force and without warning.

Two days later the French and the British, long-time friends, had not moved. Retreating Polish army units started to move through the villages. Military convoys, day and night, drove towards Skole, and Ławoczne on their way to Hungary.

The German attack was devastating, just like lava from a volcano crater. The Polish army failed the test. Police and army units were retreating, exhausted. The soldiers were sad. Their faces showed that they had not been victorious even for one day. "STRONG UNITED AND READY."

The families of the retreating uniformed policemen could be seen on the wagons as they ran away. The women and children who were with them all looked miserable.

People who arrived from Stryj a few days later said they also saw such units traveling toward Bolechów and then southeast toward Romania.

The Ukrainians, who had been dreaming of independence for a long time, thought it was the right time to take advantage of the national dream.

The Jews in the village including the Pikholtzes were trembling. Maybe their "friendly" neighbors dreamed of a Petliura as in World War I.

The Germans are Coming

In the past years the first victim of a pogrom was, for sure, the inn owner. He was considered by the crowd as evil because he asked for money for drinks and was not prepared to give his clients credit.

Regrettably the local Ukrainians could not find a Jew owning a tavern at Synowódzko as the pub was part of a shopping center called *Ukrainska Targoblah* and was owned by a Ukrainian.

In the village there was not one Jew who owned a grocery store and would give endless supplies on credit. There was no need for a specific issue to hate Jews, steal their property and even kill them.

But the fact that Jews were to blame for the crucifixion of Jesus was enough to take revenge.

So thought all those who might, G_d forbid, forget the *Pashprotnik* (Priest hierarchy) a young and anti-Semitic priest's sermons every Sunday. Recently they had been even stronger.

He was the one who handed the injured girl Dvoiraleh over to the murderous mob when she tried to look for shelter at his place of worship. This happened when the three Jewish families who had been living there for many years were killed with axes by their neighbors. In his Sunday sermon, he was the one who warned his flock of divine punishment if they tried to hide Jews.

The Jews of the village sat at home and prayed that some good spirit hung over the heads of their Polish, but mostly Ukrainian, neighbors and would not allow wicked thoughts to make way into their heads.

Grandfather Baruch sat vigilant and thought, "Who knows what has happened to his friend Isaiah Diamand, the inn owner at Lubieńce. Who knows if a crowd didn't break into the inn, loot everything and, G_d forbid, even killed him."

Ukrainians saw in the Germans not only saviors from the Polish leaders Marshal Pilsudski and Rydz Śmigły who provoked them, causing them to starve and be miserable.

Now the Germans came who not only expelled the Polish government to Romania and Hungary but who would no doubt establish an independent Ukraine.

The Pikholtz family moved to the home of a reliable Ukrainian. They stayed with him until the storm passed.

At night the sky turned red because the Germans bombed the oil refineries of Boryslav and Drohobycz. There were rumors that the Red Army had entered Poland from the east and was advancing westward.

These were the Communists who don't believe in G_d. What should we Jews ask for? Should we ask G_d that the Germans come here and impose their authority on the Ukrainians who try to hold their heads high? Or alternatively pray that the Red Army who desecrated the synagogues and churches come here?

My grandfather remembered the Austrians and the Germans during World War I "They have a culture, "Dos zenen mentchen es is do mit weymen zu gain zum tish." (They are human beings; it is possible to sit with them at the same table.) On the other hand, the Cossacks, the Bolsheviks will come riding their horses, will rob and rape and will not allow us to pray."

It was known then that the Bolsheviks closed synagogues and churches and turned them into barns and warehouses. "Die zenan awade nysht kan menczen." (These are certainly not human beings.)

Toward the end of September the armies met on both sides of the Stryj River. The atmosphere was tense and it seemed that a battle could very well start between the two armies

Urgent discussions started between the German Foreign

Office and the Soviet Union. The Germans tried to interpret the agreement according to where the two armies would meet and where the limit would stand. The Soviets thought differently and after a few days of irritation, the Soviet soldiers entered the village and the Germans retreated westward and settled on the San River.

The Soviets Get Control

The Jews used to say, "*Der Mensch tracht un der G_t Lacht*" (Men think and G_d laughs.)

As just mentioned, after two weeks of German rule, the Soviet Army entered the village. During those two weeks, the Ukrainians and the Poles of Synowódzko behaved reasonably, which was different from what the Jews expected. The Germans did not show their claws or what they were capable of.

It was not as quiet in the nearby town of Stryj. One of the first bombs landed right in the town square on the house of a Jew named Ellner. More than twenty Jews died in the basement.

Among the dead there was a distant relative of Donia named Haft. She thinks his first name was Isaac. His wife and their baby were with him but survived the bombing. They perished in the Holocaust.

As the German Army came closer to Stryj, groups of Ukrainians gathered from everywhere; riding horses, dressed in colorful Sunday clothes, to welcome the generous rescuers who no doubt would give them an independent Ukraine.

On one of the main streets they had raised a welcome triumphal arch. On the banner it read, "With Jewish skulls we will pave the way for a German victory."

The people in the Christian part of the city were cheerful while the perplexed Jews hid in their houses and cellars. The behavior of their Ukrainian neighbors, and the behavior of the Germans, showing clear signs of hatred toward the Jews. It made some of them feel pressured and that urged them to prepare themselves for the future.

One family named Morgenstern built a secret bunker for

twelve family members under their house located on Bolechówska street number 16. The bunker was equipped with everything needed for a long stay. The place was illegally connected to the municipal system of electricity, gas and water. The hidden people were able to use gas, electricity and water safely since the user could not be identified. They secretly built chimneys providing ventilation. They dug a deep hole which they used as a lavatory.

The house was given to a man named Kazik Starko to live in and it was agreed that he would provide food through the ventilation conduit and in return would get a fee. Starko set up a bakery in the building and in this way provided wheat grain and bread to those in hiding. Three times as many people hid there than had been planned.

The people hiding there used to sleep during the day and moved quietly during the night. They were cautious at all times. In the bunker many arguments and fights broke out. Most of the fights revolved around the desire to save expenses and have the other party pay, keeping more money this way for themselves for after the liberation.

One day a neighbor named Roman Bilinski came up to Starko and said, "I know you are hiding Jews in the basement."

Starko turned white and didn't know what to say. "This is the end," thought Starko. "I am going to eliminate Roman, throwing his body in the chimney downstairs. There the hiding people will drown the body in the toilet pit. Maybe someone in the house knows or saw that Roman came to me. It is impossible to conceal a person so suddenly. Maybe one of his relatives saw him coming in and not going out and I will have to eliminate him as well. Finally the Gestapo will show up, will find the bodies and the Jews hiding down there. Where will it end?" All these thoughts passed through his mind.

Roman saw Starko's embarrassment. "Don't worry, I came to warn you. At night voices are heard through the wall of your basement I came to let you know and to tell you that I want to help."

From that moment Roman Bilinski became a secret partner and helped supply food and other wares until the Jews release.

The Red Army entered Stryj in 1939 on the eve of *Yom Kippur* (The Jewish Day of Atonement, the holiest day of the year). The soldiers were greeted with mixed feelings. The Poles saw the Soviet new occupiers and it was difficult for them to hide their hatred. The Poles fought them nineteen years ago and now were fighting them again. The Polish troops had tough combat with the invaders from the east and tried to stop them until the collapse of the Polish army. Adults remembered the years 1919/1920 when the White Cossacks were there: how they pillaged and raped and how devastated the region was left when they retreated.

The Ukrainians hated the Russians even more than the Poles. They saw in the Red Army the reason for the failure to get the independence they had been longing for.

The Soviets dominated much of Eastern Ukraine and its capital Kiev since 1920. An independent Ukraine in this area? Of course not. The Soviets did not grant them independence then and would not grant it now.

At this moment they destroyed what they believed the Germans would, no doubt, give them sooner or later.

Only the Jews rejoiced. The Communists and the Jews had a good reason to rejoice. Imprisoned friends would be released immediately and they did not need to dream of a revolution in Poland or to make the Communist dream come true. The Soviets brought their bayonets for the revolution on a silver plate.

The Jewish bourgeoisie feared the loss of their property which would surely become collectivized. Still, in search of a bit of optimism, they would state, "The Soviets are better than the Germans because that bastard Hitler is 100% sure to take advantage of the Jews. And who knows if he is not preparing a pogrom on such a scale that has never been seen before." The Jews were absolutely unaware the Germans were holding back Hitler's abominable secret wicked and insane dreams.

Hitler was using physically handicapped Goebbels, who was working tirelessly on mechanisms for demonizing the Jews who were rich. Hitler also brought under German rule the Czech Republic in addition to Austria.

Orthodox Jews were the only ones who liked the Germans.

They had heard that in the Soviet Union practicing any religion was forbidden. At that time the Jews didn't know that the Soviets thought they were superior to the Germans in the respect that they would not accept Jewish life and customs. More than just property, they would also take away your soul.

Danger moved away to the west and the Jews could feel temporarily secure due to the agreement between the German Foreign Minister and his Russian counterpart. The Soviet authorities issued instructions requiring people to hand over weapons, keep shops open and there was a ban on gatherings. Food disappeared from the market and prices skyrocketed. The Stryj residents learned a new concept *Oczered* (Queuing up). Nothing could be done without standing in line.

The shopping frenzy made Soviet soldiers from the town buy anything as they were all craving good Western products. They would not test or evaluate. Everything bought was sent home right away. "Good and rich." They did not tell anyone the truth. Inside the Soviet Union people had gone hungry for twenty years.

This did not stop the Soviets feeding the people with slogans by Marx, Lenin and Stalin. "He who does not work does not eat."

This new situation caused a shortage in goods and people had to stand in line for hours, and sometimes all night, just to get a loaf of bread.

This region of Galicia was known for its important leather industry. It turned out that skins were one of the most coveted products of the Soviets.

When finally nothing could be obtained in stores, nothing but matches or *marchoka* (a kind of cheap tobacco for smoking) one joker came up with the following story:

Locomotives pulling trains eastward made a heavy sound: *Yutch Boxess, Yutch Boxess, Yutch Boxess,* (*Yutch* and *box* were a type of leather for shoes)

In Contrast, locomotive pulling trains from the East made a light sound:

Spitz'ki Machorka, Spitz'ki Machorka, Spitz'ki Machorka (matches and tobacco lighter products).

After a while commissars and their families came from within

Russia. They moved into the former administration offices and nationalized the houses of the wealthiest families in town. The commissaries installed a leadership for the local population, not respecting nationalities, party or status.

People were not really concerned with the leadership. Someone would give information about them, such as being a bourgeois in the past or exploiting others, leaving a kind of stain on a person and this person was expected to suffer in the future.

The *Bolshaja Tz'istka* methods (the Big Clean Up by Stalin in which millions of Soviet citizens were killed or languished in Siberian labor camps) would be brought to Galicia from the Soviet Union.

Residents in Stryj then discovered how to get along with the Commissaries with the help of bribes and /or corruption. "Keep helping me and I shall keep helping you."

A propos, there was a legend going on in the wake of the October Revolution, about one who saved Stalin's life. After the Revolution, Stalin gave the man a "prize," a job as a night watchman in a factory making fabrics. When the man got his first salary he realized that with this money he could not support his family. The man complained to Stalin that the job was poor and the pay so low that he could not support his family.

Stalin asked the man, "How many hours do you work at night?"

"Eight," replied the man.

"Are you awake all the time and walk around or do you take a nap occasionally?" asked Stalin.

"I sleep occasionally," the man replied.

"My friend, you need to do a better job. Open your eyes well and you will see. You will earn more," said Stalin.

That night the man was encouraged, hoping to get better wages as promised by Comrade Stalin.

Just after midnight he went on his rounds and noticed a truck approaching one of the buildings of the plant premises. The man stayed in the dark, hiding, and followed the movements of the truck. After a few moments it stopped and he noticed the plant manager. The manager unlocked the building door and a number of workers climbed out of the truck. They began to remove rolls of fabric from the factory and load them on to the truck.

The guard jumped out from where he was hiding and confronted the manager.

"What are you doing here at night?" the guard asked loudly.

The manager pulled him aside and asked him to lower his voice. He handed him a wad of money, the equivalent of two month's salary at least, and suggested that he watch another area.

The guard understood, stuffed the money into his pocket and muttered, "Long Live Comrade Stalin."

After the commissars settled and took control of the town, state institutions were established and managed trade, it provided employment. They nationalized flour mills, bakeries, factories and large businesses. Later on houses with a value above twenty thousand rubles were nationalized too.

Specialists, public activists of all kinds, and their contacts started operating. For providing bribe services the commissars estimated houses at a value lower than twenty thousand rubles. This is how quite a number of houses remained in private hands.

There were queues at bakeries. The bread itself was heavier and heavier. Importing methods from the Soviet Union, the texture was more like clay to make ceramics than what bread had been for years. In nationalized bakeries bakers had discovered the trick. Do not allow bread to remain in the oven the necessary time. The result was that the amount of flour delivered was predetermining the amount of bread. They provided the number of supposed baked bread leaving some flour for the black market.

Baked bread gets a nice colored crust but not the one insufficiently baked. A supervisor sometimes came to check the quality of the bread but getting the "Help me and I'll help you" bribe, he went away.

In the spring of 1940 the Soviets abolished the use of the Polish *złoty*. Only the *ruble* was recognized as the legal currency. A few days prior to this, the very same management paid salaries to all employees of Eastern Poland in *złoty*. Due to this sudden decree the population remained without means of payment.

A flow of thousands of Jewish refugees, *bieżnicy*, arrived in town from the western part of Poland. A few found work but the majority moved eastward. (The author thought that interestingly; the flow of refugees was not questioned and made people think they, themselves, would be saved a year and nine months later.)

In the summer of 1940 the authorities brutally expelled all the *bieżnicy* refugees and sent them to Siberia. This move included those who had a regular job in the city. This brutal decision was made at night. The candidates were ordered to be ready in twenty minutes with their belongings. In fact, this saved their lives. There were cases of children separated from their parents or women from their husbands. People were home when the special brigade arrived; catching and deporting the *bieżnicy*. They were separated using force.

But the Soviets didn't send only the *bieżnicy* to Siberia. They also sent the rich factory owners and others recommended by "friends" as someone who had exploited the working class or the poor farmers.

Now the Soviets taught the new citizens what Communism really was. In this group were refugees from the lowest working class who had no property. They were able to go and, retrospectively, this saved their lives. The factory or mansion owners were deported. Now they were all poor together, rich or destitute, mostly Jews, Poles and Ukrainians were transported in freight cars that had been prepared in advance.

The cars were equipped with bunks and heaters forewarning a long journey. Trains headed east and north for weeks and months. Long journeys. Many people died on the way due to the bitter northern cold and the lack of warm suitable clothing as well as the lack of food. It simply wasn't available.

Eastern Galicia became part of the Ukrainian Republic and Ukrainian became the official language. This decision triggered the indignation of the Poles who, after twenty years of independence,were again under the rule of a foreign conqueror.

Local Ukrainians were not assigned management positions before the war. It was not possible to find enough experienced administrators. Therefore the authorities had no alternative. They offered key positions to Poles and Jews.

The Farm is Confiscated and the
Pikholtz Family Moves to Stryj

Although the farm did not belong to the Pikholtz family, years of dedicated management and contact with the local population left the impression among the neighbors that they were the farm's owners.

If the neighbors thought that then, for the Communists, they are *Kulaky* (farm owners) and exploiters sucking the blood from poor farmers. As a punishment they should be sent to Siberia.

The Pikhotzes were aware that the farm would be nationalized. In order to avoid their possible deportation to Siberia, an idea that scared all the mentally sane, the Pikholtzes left the village and settled in Stryj. It was done in the first few days of the Soviet takeover of the region and long before the inspector showed up and nationalized the farm.

The farm remained in the hands of the dedicated employees. When the war came to an end, everything would go back into place. They expected to be rewarded for their good care.

It was the time of the harvest. The orchards were full of ripening fruit. There was no landlord. And there is no need to store the grain. Harvest, reap and take it home. What more do you need? What will happen later is G_d's problem. At the moment thank G_d for his generosity.

To ensure their living in Stryj, father Mathes asked an employee who worked on the farm for many years as a horseman and who was one of the trustees, to come during the night bringing two milking cows. The faithful worker walked all night to Stryj and brought the cows.

At grandmother Taube's house there was a large warehouse in the yard where grandfather kept merchandise. He was a merchant.

Since 1937, when Grandfather David Samuel died, the warehouse was empty and abandoned. This warehouse Donia's father converted into an apartment where they settled.

Near the new apartment her father built a barn and the cows were kept there. The children now were engaged in chores. They had to bring grass for the cows and they learned to milk them.

"He who does not work does not eat." The population was forced to learn these key words and practice them. Under Soviet rule all must work somewhere. Father Mathes, an Orthodox Jew, found himself a job as a security guard at the laundry. In this job he was able to keep up the tradition and not work on Saturday.

Grandfather Baruch, an elderly man, did not work. He devoted himself to daily prayers and to keeping the traditions. Since they had moved to Stryj, grandfather and Donia's father attended the yellow synagogue next to their new home.

On Saturdays they dressed in black suits and a *shtreimel* as is the honorable tradition of Czortków *Hasidim*. They would pray for better times and for being saved.

In the beginning the authorities decided not to interfere in the religious life of the residents. Institutions that provided religious needs, and who were depending on a budget, had difficulties and were forced to restrain their spending and were supported only by the community.

The Jewish residents hoped to get help from the pre-war Jewish Communists. But the Communists didn't help at all.

The Yiddish language that was spoken before by these Communists, and now recognized by the authorities, was suddenly forgotten and replaced by Ukrainian to flatter the ruler.

The *minyan* (a quorum of ten men required for a collective prayer) organized on Saturdays and holidays were expected to be declared an invalid assembly. Even worse, underground praying participants were expecting to be sent to Siberia.

Donia's younger sister Gittel went back to the same Pedagogiczna School she had attended. Yitzhakl, the youngest child in the Pikholtz family, joined the boys elementary school named after the Polish poet Mickewicz.

After school and after their homework was done, the children helped in the house. The oldest girl Libke got a part-time job as a bookkeeper and the rest of the day helped her mother at home and took care of the two cows.

Donia never went back to school. The sixteen year old, who was still not obliged to carry an ID card, decided to take advantage of the situation and got into the black market to help support her family.

Since Donia was, up to that time, entitled to attend school, she went to the largest town of the district of Lwów as if she was a student. An acquaintance of her parents, a Jewish tanner named Berger whose tannery had been nationalized, was hiding a large stock of skins. He was selling them on the black market in Lwów.

Three times a week Donia would take some skins from Stryj. She carried a school bag holding two textbooks and several notebooks. She wrapped a skin around her body, wearing a blouse and a big skirt and a Ukrainian shawl over her head. This is how the plumpish student went "to school."

In Lwów Donia removed the skin and handed it to the man representing Mr. Berger and got paid for the service. Before returning home from Lwów she used to buy socks and other things lacking in Stryj at the local market. She haggled toughly with the traders operating in the black market. Usually she was able to lower the price. Donia once even brought back some marmalade made in Rumania.

The same goods she brought back to Stryj, father Mathes would sell at a substantial profit. These were the first lessons Donia learned at the Faculty of Resourcefulness: The Everyday Life University. Donia decided to laureate with honors and excellence.

Germans Attack on June 22, 1941
The Tragedy Begins

The easy life didn't last long. The Germans prepared a surprise for the Soviets similar to the one they'd prepared for the Poles only 21 months before.

On the 22nd of June 1941 the Germans attacked with a blitz along the Soviet Union border. The town of Lwów was heavily bombed and many houses were left in rubble. A few days later the town was surrounded by the German Army and attacked without restraint. The German beast came close to Stryj as well.

The Poles were apathetic. The Ukrainians were joyful. Now their dream was coming true. This time the Germans would stay long enough to establish a Ukrainian independent state.

The Jews fell into depression. They were once again on the verge of disaster. So far they had become accustomed to not knowing what tomorrow would bring. Now more disruption was in the offing.

The Jews prayed to G_d, the same G_d the Soviets did not recognize. They prayed that the "Invincible" Red Army, as the propaganda used to say, would muster its courage and resist the Germans. But such a miracle didn't happen.

Thursday, the 22nd of June 1941 Donia remembers well. German planes flew overhead and bombed the railway station and the military airport near the town of Stryj. The "Invincible" Soviet Army retreated in a panic similar to what the Polish Army had done less than two years before. But this time the army retreated in trucks. Soldiers on foot could also be seen.

The Soviet military technology was superior to that of the Poles in 1939. A damaged truck was pushed into a rain ditch and set on fire. The soldiers from the damaged truck were given a lift by men in other trucks that passed by in a continuous flow. The retreating soldiers would pick up civilians who wanted to run away with them to the east.

A week after the German assault on the Soviet Union, the Soviets left Stryj. Individuals who were party members, or known Communists before the war, were getting ready to flee to the east with the Red Army as it began to retreat. Senior officials in the short period of Soviet rule were also preparing to flee to the east.

For some in the Jewish population the decision to flee was made partly due to rumors that came from the Poles. Relatives told them about the Warsaw Ghetto and of the trimming of beards and wigs of the religious Jews. These acts performed by Germans in uniform on the streets of Warsaw had been observed and left no room for optimism. The Poles even reported cases of murder.

But for most Jews these were only rumors and they were difficult to believe. Those who didn't want to move didn't listen.

They thought, "Worse it cannot be." Everyone remembered the sleepless nights expecting a knock on the door. The Orthodox people didn't think of running away.

After a few days, when there were fewer and fewer trains, some one hundred Jews took their last chance and boarded overloaded trains with the retreating movement going eastward.

Several hundred young Jews were drafted into the army and some of them had the luck to survive. Among the extended Pikholtz family, only Donia's cousin Isaac fled with the Red Army. He knew that being a member of the Communist Youth Movement, *Komsomol*, if he stayed in his town, the Ukrainians or the Germans would kill him.

For the past two years the Orthodox Jews had kept up with their religious traditions. They thought the Germans would allow them to observe the Commandments. They would not have to practice underground. Just a year and a half ago they left the village to avoid being sent to the polar bears; Siberia.

Now, after settling in Stryj, they met neighbors and friends. They were accepted in the congregation. They had no reason to run away again. They were not going to move anywhere else. Although they heard the Germans might not behave decently to Jewish people, they didn't expect it to be any worse than it had been for the past two years.

Donia thinks that maybe her grandparents and parents thought "good riddance" when the last Soviet troops left Stryj.

The new Red Army recruits were those who had not yet had a taste of the war. They were from the area and didn't want to be far from home. They didn't want to withdraw deep into Russia with the army. They didn't want to fight. They wanted to be home and keep up with their studies. They abandoned their units, putting down their arms and walking home.

Those poor people who had no civilian clothes waited for the Nationalist Ukrainian gangs holding yellow and blue strips of fabric showing their affiliation. These Nationalists carried thick sticks and beat the new recruits, murdering them. They pleaded that they had been recruited against their will, and that they escaped because they didn't want to serve the Communists.

But it didn't help. Every word was accompanied by a deluge of blows. After murdering their victim, the criminals checked their victim's pockets and split the profits between themselves. They also removed the shoes from the dead bodies. The same fate was met by small groups of the Red Army who had abandoned their units. The rain ditches along the road were filled with the bodies of these soldiers.

Slovakian and Hungarian army units entered the town of Stryj and remained there for about three weeks.

The Jews were confused. Rumors spread that before withdrawing the Soviets murdered a number of Ukrainians, Poles, and Zionist activists and kept the bodies in the prison of the town. The bodies were found in the cellar of the prison. They were covered with lime. The presence of the bodies of Jews did not prevent the Ukrainians from carrying out a pogrom. They murdered more Jews from the town.

As a response to the finding of corpses, a major demonstration was organized, especially by the Ukrainian population out of resentment against the Soviet regime in Stryj. Thousands of residents of Stryj and the surrounding areas attended the mass funeral which become a disaster for the Jews of this town.

Groups of Ukrainian thugs began a rampage through the town. They broke into apartments where Jews lived. The men were dragged to the Christian cemetery and there they were savagely beaten.

The Jews brought to the cemetery were ordered to dig graves for the victims. Diggers were beaten while digging and feared they would be dropped into the graves together with the corpses.

Because the war broke out unexpectedly there were many people who were away from home. On their way back they encountered groups of Ukrainian rioters who murdered them after identifying them as Jews. Individual survivors from nearby villages, some of whom were injured, told about the pogrom and atrocities performed by their Ukrainian neighbors.

After the free hand for actions granted to the Ukrainians against the Jews, the Nazis decided to restrain them. The Ukrainians were ordered to operate only when receiving orders from the authorities. The authority's plan at that time was secret. The Germans wanted to be the ones to manage the blood bath.

After a few cases of abuse and murder, which at first seemed like the end of the world, much worse began to happen. The older people, who had been suffering in their lives, came up with the following statement: "A human being is stronger than iron."

In July 1941 a rumor spread in Stryj that the Gestapo had a list of alleged Communist party members to be executed. The list reported that twelve Jews had been caught and had been executed in the village of Grabowce not far from Stryj. The Germans also took another Jewish group to help dig the grave for the twelve people sentenced to death.

The moment they entered the town, the Germans triggered the mechanism of Nazi atrocities against the Jewish population.

Jews were required, according to the German directives, to choose a *Judenrat* (a council of Jews whose duty was to fulfill the German's orders). One of their first duties was to establish a census of the Jewish population. The second duty was to establish an employment exchange and provide day-to-day Jews for forced slave labor, especially for repugnant work.

The *Judenrat* was committed to yield to all the demands of the Nazis. Oscar Huterer was its head. Together with the *Judenrat*, a Jewish police force was set up. Most were hated by the Jews because they blindly followed the German orders.

The Jewish police and the *Judenrat* deluded themselves. They hoped that by fulfilling the German's orders it would save them even though it required doing things that were immoral and contrary to their conscience.

Some Jewish policemen helped the Jews by warning them. The only reward for both groups was their execution later on.

A flood of instructions and notices came forth one after the other. "Our war is against the Communist enemy." "Citizens, regardless of your religion, we Germans warranty peace and order."

Almost the same day an announcement from the City Military Commander was declared. "Jews must turn in their phones and radios. Those who do not comply with this directive will be punished by State of Emergency Laws."

All Jews were ordered to prepare a white band for themselves in the middle of which they would paint or embroider a blue Star of David. The band had to be no less than seven centimeters (more than three inches) wide and the Star of David no smaller than six centimeters (about 2.5 inches) high.

Jewish women prepared the bands using the cuffs of shirt sleeves or spare stiff collars. (In those times shirt sleeves as well as collars were removable and could be changed without changing the whole shirt.) All Jews had to wear this band with the blue Star of David on their right arm.

The German officers from different headquarters brought their families to Stryj and the Judenrat had to provide furnished apartments upon their request.

The Jewish police confiscated furniture, rugs and home equipment. First, things were confiscated from wealthy Jews. Later on middle and lower class Jews were also pillaged. They thought, "Better give property than your soul."

Jews were ordered to register at the Labor Office and were employed as forced labor in the factories around town. Under the Soviet occupation the unofficial slogan was, "He who does not work does not eat." Under the German occupation the unofficial slogan was, "He who does not work dies."

Even before the *Judenrat* was established Germans confiscated Jewish businesses and their owners received no compensation. The cows of the Pikholtzes, which they wisely moved to Stryj from the Synowódzko Niżne farm two years before, were confiscated by the German administration. Even the laundry was confiscated where Donia's father had worked since the Russian period.

The *Judenrat* opened several shops where the Jewish population were provided with meager rations. The rations were not enough to sustain life and the Jewish population began to starve to death. They began selling their remaining furniture and valuable clothing to the Christians for food.

The cost of living became terribly high. The price of food products was skyrocketing. The farmers who had brought their crops for sale demanded more money.

Small murders were happening. A single man, or a group of Jews, were murdered for all kind of reasons or pretext such as a denunciation by their Ukrainian neighbors about a statement condemning the Germans during the Soviet rule or some unfair treatment against a Ukrainian working in a factory when a Jew was in charge.

Here's an excerpt from Jonah Friedler, Donia's uncle, as it appears in the Stryj *Yizkor Book* (Book of Remembrance). "On the second day of the Stryj German occupation, a German soldier came to my apartment accompanied by a Ukrainian thug who served as a snitch and would point out where Jewish homes were. I recognized this guy as the servant at the bathhouse. He used to sleep there. I was called to work and was ordered to take along a bucket, a broom and rags. On the street I joined the Jews who were already taken from their homes. We were lead to the town square to clean tanks and collect bricks from the bombed houses and set them into equal piles. Work was not boring at all because the German supervisor often beat us. He would whip our head and our back. Ukrainian hooligans stood there enjoying the show and made fun of us. I dared to ask the supervisor why I was beaten. Did I not work according to the instructions? I didn't have time to finish my sentence when the German whipped my face, cursing me in a vocabulary impossible to translate. Blood was running all over my face. The next day I was appointed by the Jewish police to work at the train station. We carried all kinds of bolts, wheels and heavy metal tools on our shoulders. At work I met a young high official on the train, a Ukrainian who knew me from the good times. He said, "You have sucked our blood. The chicken and fattened geese the Ukrainian peasant sold you while they settled for a bread meal you sold him. Jews have always lived in luxury. All houses in our city are yours. "*Miasto Nasze a domy wasze.*" It is our city but the houses are yours. Ukrainian hands built them. We have always been your slaves, doormen, or brushed your shoes and emptied your toilets. You wear the most beautiful expensive clothes. You have lived in the most beautiful apartments. You have eaten our bread and drank our water. Now it is time to repay the debt. With your life you will pay."

(Note from the author: As I previously mentioned, in 1996 I conducted a Root Finding Group of 40 people from all over the world to my home town of Bolechów. We stopped in Stryj which is about 20 km north of Bolechów. The group was accompanied by a number of psychologists and psychiatrists from the USA and Switzerland. The trip was escorted by German radio and TV crews and helped by a 25 year old student, a Ukrainian woman from the University of Lwów. After three days of the tour the TV team and the psychologist asked the interpreter her opinion of what she had experience and seen; the mass graves, the prayers and the testimonies. She answered in one sentence, "Well it was known the Jews were rich."

Should the Jews be blamed for being better educated and more efficient? Consequently they got the popular jobs in Austrian ruled Galicia before WWI. Sometimes the anti-Semitic Polish government between the wars gave the Jews the better jobs. The Polish government that was known to have an anti-Semitic approach still relied on the skills of Jews rather than those of the Ukrainians. Should Jews be guilty for saving money for education when the Ukrainians left their salaries in taverns and had no money left for education? Did that justify the hatred of both the Poles and the Ukrainians toward the Jews? Or, on the contrary, should it have served as an example of good behavior? What can be said about people whose majority was illiterate? People signed documents using fingerprints or by marking a cross instead of a signature. How was it possible to see the difference between a cross and another cross? (Graphologists were quite busy in those times.)

The Jewish Quarter

Toward the end of 1941 an order was published: that a Jewish quarter would be established. This was the first step before creating a ghetto. A number of blocks or sections, most of which had been lived in by Jews for generations, were chosen. This was the beginning of the physical separation between Jews and Aryans. Jews living in Aryan neighborhoods were ordered to move into the Jewish quarter and were pushed into houses and apartments of the Jews who lived there before.

The implementation of this transfer, and the allocation of houses, was performed by the *Judenrat* with the help of the *Ordnung Dienst,* the Jewish Police. This action caused an unbearable human density. At that time about 12,000 Jews were living in Stryj. The Germans in 1942 didn't see a problem bringing in 11,000 more Jews from nearby towns to live there.

The apartments were equipped with three tier bunks in order to accommodate so many people. Due to the crowding and poor sanitary conditions, diseases started to break out. The Germans had planned in advance. They immediately began easing the system by making more severe cuts.

(Author's note. The legend of *Passover* is told. Pharaoh, King of Egypt, imposed on the children of Israel harsh decrees. As the decrees were more severe, the children of Israel multiplied and prospered.)

There were Germans who knew the *Torah*; Adolf Eichman for example. The story of the Exodus had not escaped their knowledge. These criminals who controlled the Nazi Party wanted to upset the Jews to test the G_d of Israel.

They did it in various towns. Where the Jewish population was the hardest hit, ordained rabbis preached before the miserable public that the G_d of Israel had no power or influence over the course of history. The Nazis brutally demonstrated with confidence that the story of the Exodus and the various plagues were nice stories but only that, stories.

Aktions are a systematic elimination of people after suffering humiliation and torture all of which precisely followed the German order. If the *aktion* was supposed to kill 1,000 Jews started at 5 AM and was supposed to end at 12 noon; if a Jew was caught after this time he was set free and sent home to wait for the next *aktion*. With the same sense of organization, if the quota of 1,000 Jews was obtained before noon, the *aktion* was over.

Jews who worked in factories outside the Jewish Quarter possessed work permits allowing them to leave the Quarter. And Christians were allowed to enter the Jewish Quarter for work.

Plan of the Stryj Ghetto

The *Aktions*

On August 22, 1941, the Germans carried out, with the help of the Ukrainian police, the first *aktion* in Stryj. Out of the total population of Jews in Stryj they took the first 1,000 of them among the intelligentsia and the leadership of the Stryj Jewish community. They held them in the City Hall where they were beaten, cruelly tortured and some were even killed on the premises. Those who remained alive were kept for two weeks in a muddy field. They were tortured all the time and not allowed to drink or eat. About a hundred of these Jewish detainees were able to escape after bribing the guards. Seven days later the remaining Jews were taken close to the Hołobutów Forest and, after digging their own graves, they were murdered.

Quotation from the testimony of Isaac Nussenblatt: Massacre of Thousands of Jews from Stryj as it appears in the Stryj *Yizkor Book* (Book of Remembrance). "After the barbaric acts of violence, the murdering of individuals or groups, the destruction of the Jews of Stryj reached another stage: the killing of thousands Jews. It was a night of horrors in September 1941. (This date is controversial.) No one could imagine that this might have happened and that the Germans and their vile, barbaric collaborators murdered women, children and innocent people. On this terrifying night, as everyone was fast asleep, hundreds of German police, Ukrainians and Gestapo members, all armed from head to toe, performed these cold-blooded murders the details of which had been well planned in advance. Brutally abused and without a hint of pity, men, women and children were driven out of their beds. The Jews had not yet understood there was a need to prepare for shelter and hideouts in order to avoid incarceration in the Trybunalska Street prison. Hundreds of prisoners were held in the yard of the Ukrainian police station on Batorego Street and many were tortured to death. While in jail, the Jews were watched mainly by the Ukrainian police. Some Jews managed to get away using bribery and later on told of severe torture in the prison cells. At night the Ukrainian police would storm the cells and beat the prisoners without mercy, sometimes killing them. The beaten and the injured were not helped medically and, consequently, many died. Victims were buried on the premises of the prison. After seven days of abuse and torture the Jews were taken to an unknown place. The local police returned in the evening of the same day and discovered the place where the poor prisoners had been slaughtered. It was five kilometers away from Stryj in the village of Rilov in the Hołobutów Forest.

The monument in the Hołobutów Forest

"Those who bribed their way out of prison also described the appalling scenes when people were executed. Among the victims who perished, executed in that group of 1,000 are the following, forever in my memory: the lawyers Rosenberg, and also Milk Spiegel; Isaac Hobel; the brothers Joseph and Hesio Caisler; Donek Sandberg, Irka Ellner, Samuel Brauner Sonia Reichman, David Nussenblatt, Moshe Kron, Yaakov Bar, Mania Walker, Herman Zoldan, Oscar Reiner.

"I was employed at the *Strassenbauamt* (The Office for Road Paving) and occasionally I was in the village of Rilov collecting testimonies from farmers who approved of the brutal murders by the Ukrainian police. I wanted to go to the grave where the unfortunate brothers were killed but I was warned that going

83

there was punishable by death."

Donia remembered this *aktion*. She said: "After taking these 1,000 Jews, authorities slyly told the Jewish population to bring food to the prisoners. But in fact they were already buried in Hołobutów. Among those killed by the murderers of that *aktion* was the first victim of the Pikholtz family. It was Dad's brother Uncle Fishel. His wife Pepka came to us and said, "They took Fishel at work."

The poor woman didn't know, or didn't want to know, the truth. Fishel didn't return. Pepka was left with two small children.

Donia doesn't remember if these 1,000 Jews were gathered according to a list.

(Author's note: Presumably they were because that was the procedure in all of the town's first *aktions*.)

Donia also remembered that, after some time, letters arrived from those who had been murdered telling their families that they were fine. But the families realized that the handwriting was not that of their loved ones. However, Donia said they all lived with hope and wanted to believe their loved ones were actually working somewhere. We didn't know it was just a pretext. The worst was yet to come.

Donia said she learned of Hołobutów only after the Liberation in 1944.

After the first *aktion* people began to search frantically for a place to hide. The Jews started building bunkers in their basements, attics, out-houses and courtyards. Imagination and resourcefulness guided people to find hiding places. Basements were reduced in size thanks to a fake wall. Camouflaged doors were built in attics, under mangers, above toilet ceilings, outhouses and even in sewers. Everything was built and camouflaged with intelligence hoping it would not catch a German's eye or that of the collaborators.

Steps were taken to prevent the German trained dogs from discovering these hiding places. To confuse the dog's sense of smell, the Jews used oil and black pepper which they scattered or sprayed before entering the hiding place.

In most cases one of the most difficult problems was how to

camouflage the entrance to the secret place after the last person entered it. There were several methods to conceal the way into the hiding place. One family member would be left out and would hide himself in another small hideout prepared in advance.

Another method was, in the lowest and darkest place they would remove a number of bricks and crawl inside through the opening. They carefully put back the bricks one by one, leaving no trace of the fake wall. Sometimes the fake wall was completed without a mark or a detail amiss and totally matched the original wall around it.

In these cases the entrance to the hiding place was from the bottom, through the floor in the next room through parquet boards. In Galicia most floors were made of oak wood boards which always had narrow slots between them. They were usually attached with nails that could not be seen from the outside. The boards were approximately 30 centimeters wide and one meter long. They were painted brown or red. One such board, in a dark place in a room or under the table, was removed as an entrance to the cellar's hideout.

Sometimes the hiding place itself or the entrance was from a building that served as a warehouse for scrap or a reserve for fire wood. The most popular method in building a hiding place was to have shelves facing the outside room. And on these shelves were all kinds of jars, household tools, baskets and more. The entire wall rotated on an axis. Because of the shelves it was difficult to see there was a fake wall.

Almost without exception it was not possible to stay too long in these hideouts. They hideouts saved people during the *aktion* for a day or two. But they didn't offer a long-term solution nor answer the main problem of how to survive.

The Jewish Quarter, over time, became a ghetto that was separated from the Aryan districts by wooden fences, barbed wire or walls of buildings that had no windows.

The established *Judenrat* provided different things to please the Germans running the city. In addition they yielded to the demands of soldiers and officers of the *Sonder Kommando SD* (Special Unit whose duty was the extermination of the Jews in occupied territories) and occasionally confiscated Jewish properties on their own for themselves.

The fall of 1941 was very rainy and later on the winter was unusually cold. Shortages began to be felt by the Pikholtz family. A small allowance of sticky and heavy flat bread per person, per day, for which you had to queue up for hours, was not enough to satisfy the hungry family. The Pikholtzes started selling things from home in order to buy wheat. It had to dry and be milled. The porridge that was cooked with this coarse flour, eaten with bread was somehow satisfactory, or at least filled their bellies even if it didn't provide adequate nutrition.

The family's watches were the first items to be sold. Then it was the turn of the furniture. For the beautiful sideboard the Pikholtzes bought less than two years before from a German family who had been exiled to the west by the Soviets they received 20 kilos of grain.

The family slowly let its assets go. Little was left to sell. Father Mathes and Grandfather Baruch felt lucky to get work at the *Judenrat*. For a paltry sum they had to go through the ghetto streets and load the dead bodies of members of the community onto their carriage. These people had died of hunger or illness and it was Father Mathes and Grandfather Baruch's job to bring them to the cemetery for burial.

Sometimes in the evening, after eating their plate of porridge and praying thankfully to G_d for the food they had eaten, they would tell of an important person of the community who was buried that very same day. The man was so thin it was difficult to recognize him.

These innocent anxious people looked up to Heaven, murmuring grace and a prayer to the Lord for helping them survive the day and keep them at night.

Young people who were able to work were stopped on the street and sent to the labor camp of the "SS."

The *Sonder Kommando* personnel often carried out small eliminations. They would hold a small group of twenty or thirty Jews, take them to the woods where they would be killed. One day you would be here, the next you would be gone forever.

The remaining family members would go to the *Judenrat* to ask where their loved ones were and were told that, according to their information, they had been sent to forced labor. Presumably the *Judenrat* knew what had occurred to certain groups; that they were murdered. But they were not allowed to reveal the truth to avoid causing a panic.

Laws against the Jews were so Draconian it would be hard to describe them. Jews who had committed the slightest offense against German laws were arrested and executed.

The winter of 1941 was difficult, but not only for the Jews who were cold and hungry. It was also difficult for the well-fed Germans who were on the eastern front.

German soldiers and their Italian allies were not used to the intense cold. Hitler apparently ignored, or did not dwell on, the reasons for Napoleon's defeat in Russia. As with Napoleon's armies, it is now the invincible army of the *Fuhrer* that could not cope with the Russian winter. German soldiers born in the Rhine and Mozel areas, or their allies the Austrians and the Italians felt the real cold for the first time. Their tank engines, the artillery draggers and the soldiers themselves were freezing. They did not want to leave the trenches or the buildings where they had settled.

The German people of the *Reich* volunteered to send their furs for the soldiers on the eastern front. The fur idea was immediately applied to the Jews who were required to hand over all their furs. The order was that the Jews of Stryj must bring their furs to the headquarters of the city within two days.

The *Judenrat* undertook the coordination of the fur collection and delivered the furs to the authorities. The *Judenrat* notified all the Jews in Stryj of this new requirement.

The Jews who had not sold their furs, or did not make a secret of owning them, brought their old tattered fur coats to the *Judenrat*. Their best and most precious furs were handed to their Christian acquaintances for hiding until the storm passed. All was based on friendship without any contract or written agreement.

The Jews would drown their furs in the ditches of the

outhouse rather than give them to the murderers.

But the German and Ukrainian police did not wait until the Jews brought them their furs. They started searching on their own; entering the houses of the Jews and collecting all their precious furs. Only some of them were given to the German headquarters. The most expensive furs they kept for themselves. These fur coats later on could be purchased on the Black Market of Lwów and Kraków. The Ukrainian authorities reported every case where a Jew was seen hiding a coat in his possession. There was a case when a Jew paid with his life for trying to do this.

The Ukrainians were happy whenever they heard of a victory on the German side when dealing with the Jews because it meant a small or large *aktion* and looting would follow.

Reduction of the Jewish Quarter

In the middle of the harsh Polish winter, when the temperature reached minus 15 Celsius (five degrees Fahrenheit) the *Judenrat* was ordered to bring an expulsion injunction regarding all non-productive elements, such as the unemployed, because they were not fit for the jobs in the ghetto or other places outside. It included widows or women whose husbands had been mobilized by the Red Army.

About 500 people were put in carts accompanied by Ukrainian police and Germans on horseback. The poor Jews were taken into the Carpathian Mountains to a very remote place, where farmers before the war constantly suffered from hunger. The German authorities chose that remote place because they clearly knew that people would not have a chance to find food. And without food and any heating in the cold winter all the Jews deported there would die.

Indeed this is what happened. A few weeks later a few individuals with swollen bodies due to hunger, wrapped in rags and covered in cold sores, came back.

The German authorities were given to understand, and had begun to accustom the Christian population, that Jewish life has no value. Municipal trucks or those in private hands bore signs reading "Death to the Jews."

Offending cartoons were showing up on many walls with images of Jews taking advantage of the Aryans. One example of this was a drawing of a fat Jew with a long curved nose. He was wearing a heavy gold chain leading to a gold watch sticking out from his waistcoat pocket and many dollars flowing out of his pockets. He was stepping on a poor Aryan. The bottom line of the cartoon read," The mighty German Army will bring this to an end."

Images with slogans, posters and cartoons encouraged the Ukrainians to understand the situation with no need to read the caption since many of them didn't know how to read and could not wait until the powerful German Army would end it. They wanted to get rid of the Jews so they could steal their property.

As a result of these cartoons and slogans and more, the Ukrainian Nationalists attacked Jewish groups who worked out of town or on their way back home from work. Some trouble makers ordered Jews to take off their clothes and shoes and would leave them only in their underwear. These attacks were accompanied by severe beatings and even murders. They beat mostly those who refused to undress or those who had spare clothes or items in their pockets.

Many Jews worked in various factories in the city and the countryside around it.

At the same time the Germans ordered the *Judenrat* to provide personnel every day for public chores. It included all sorts of menial jobs such as cleaning septic tanks and latrines. In order to humiliate the Jews, they were forced to fulfill these tasks with their bare hands, not allowing them to add the necessary gloves, mops or brushes to the buckets.

Some people couldn't stand the smell. It made them vomit or faint. Those who fainted at work never returned home and were never heard from again.

The Orthodox Jews were waiting for a miracle which was in no hurry to reveal itself. Even on the brink of death, some seconds before the bullet broke the tether keeping them alive, they believed in a miracle and expected it.

It was said that in one small *aktion* after the establishment of the ghetto, the Germans discovered that most apartments were empty. The Jews had hidden themselves and were hard to find.

The Germans became very angry. "How come these damned Jews are hiding and making our work difficult?"

The Germans were furious. They intended to search an apartment. To their surprise the Jewish family was not hiding. The owner of the apartment showed them a Turkish passport. The German officer ripped it up saying, "You don't need a passport anymore. Turkey will not wage war against Germany because of a few Turkish Jews."

The Jewish hospital was full to the brim. It hid patients who knew the doctors. The "hospitalized" thought the Germans would not enter this place because it was well know that the Germans were afraid of disease. They thought that being in the hospital gave them immunity. The Germans entered the hospital and shot dead everyone lying in a bed.

After this *aktion* the Jews felt lost. Even the most optimistic lost hope. People walked with their heads bowed; their faces grey with continual fear.

In the ghetto there was a constant movement of men and women looking for their lost loved ones.

To help support her family, and be productive, Donia decided to take advantage of her understanding of the types of animal skins and to use the experience she had acquired during the Soviet era and when she traveled to Lwów.

Donia went to the tannery once belonging to the Jew named Berger in order to ask for a job. She said: "I worked very hard and kept thinking how I could make myself less of a burden. I noticed that the factory had a lot of unused land. I suggested to the Ukrainian plant manager *Reichsdeutche* (of German origin) to use the undeveloped area for a garden. I could grow vegetables. The manager agreed and I used the experience with growing plants I had acquired in my childhood. I turned the ground, hoed it and made a number of beds ready to receive the seeds or seedlings. The manager brought me different seeds which I planted. The soil was remarkably fertile and grew a crop of vegetables of exceptional quality. Occasionally, on my way home, the manager would send me to his wife in Stryj to deliver fresh vegetables that I'd just picked. I arranged with my mother to wait for me on the way and would give her some of the vegetables. The idea of a vegetable garden was great. I was released earlier from work. I went to town with the vegetables. And the work in the garden was much easier than the work in the tannery.

"The boss and his wife were decent people. Every time I brought vegetables to his wife she gave me a piece of bread. This way I earned twice as much."Donia, like the other twenty or so Jewish workers, wore a patch with the letter W and a serial number on it. Some Jews interpreted the W as the initial letter of an important German word *Wichtig*. Others interpreted this letter as the initial letter of *Wehrmacht* (Army). Either way, all those who had to wear this letter began to believe it was their salvation. The letter W was to point out the importance of the subject and their contribution to the German war effort.

Donia said that on an early summer day in 1942, while she was going to work early in the morning, everything around seemed quiet. No unusual tension had been felt for days. Oh how different the situation was a few hours later.

"When I was on my way home in the early afternoon with some vegetables for the plant manager's wife, as was my custom, I was suddenly trapped in a small *aktion*. I was caught with the vegetables in my hands. This was a double fault. First I was Jewish and second I was smuggling food into the ghetto.

"They gathered about 300 of us in the prison building. I explained to the Ukrainian police that I was productive and pointed to the letter W attached to my shirt with a safety pin. I pointed out to the policemen who arrested me that I was assigned to deliver the vegetables to the wife of my plant manager, a Ukrainian of German descent, and that I had to return to work.

"When I saw my request was not answered and they were not ready to release me I asked that they inform my boss that I couldn't return to work because I was arrested. I told them I didn't want him to be angry with me. The merciful policeman told my boss I was with them.

"Meanwhile, the boss's wife, who knew I was supposed to come with the vegetables, seeing I didn't show up, called her husband asking what had happened. My boss arrived in his buggy and shouted at the Ukrainian police that they are not supposed to arrest me because I was wearing the W and that my work was essential. They let me go.

"The rest of the group was taken somewhere but to this day we have no idea where. They may have been murdered in the Hołobutów Forest or sent to Bełżec. I think they were killed in the Hołobutów Forest as this is where the Germans murdered the first 1,000 Jews of Stryj. The Bełżec death camp was not known at the time."

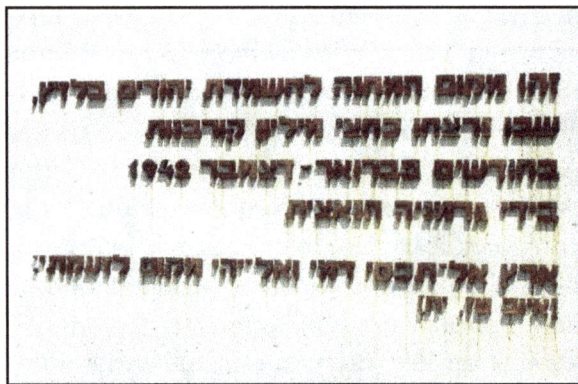

One of the marble stones with iron letters
at the entrance to the Bełżec museum

"My boss was good to me because I also worked in his house on Saturdays and Sundays. I cleaned his pigsty. They appreciated the fact that I was hard working and conscientious.

The Big *Aktion* and the
Jump from the Death Train

The Germans chose the ideal time for their *aktion*. Being aware of the Jewish holiday's dates and customs, they chose this particular time of penitence between *Rosh Hashana* and *Yom*

Kippur when Jews pray and hope for miracles to happen.

On September 17-18 in 1942 they organized the Great *Aktion*. Many teams of German police, Ukrainian police and *Wafen SS* surrounded the ghetto. The side streets were guarded by the *Baudienst* (Polish Building Services). The search was carried out with the help of the Jewish police. The criminals were looking for valuables belonging to the Jews while taking the people out of their hiding places.

The Jews were surprised at the beginning of the *aktion*. Those who had nowhere to hide, or didn't have time to get into hiding places, hid as they could under a bed, in a closet, in an attic or a basement. Everyone in a hiding place was hoping for a chance to postpone the worst.

The Jews found by the murderers were brought to the *rynek*, (the town square) where they stayed under the observation of the *Obermentsch* (super human being) the top men of the SS. There were countless selections. Finally everyone who, in the opinion of the SS, was unfit for work, was put in groups of four and marched to the railway station.

Jews were hiding anywhere they could, even in the sewage system, trying to find a shelter from the *aktion*. This great *aktion* lasted for three days.

In October the Germans carried out another *aktion* similar in number to the previous one and organized by the very same people. About 4,000 Jews were sent to the death camp in Bełżec.

Donia kept telling me, "This time we were all attacked by German military units, the Gestapo, the *Shupo* and the *Kripo* with the armed Ukrainian police. As they had learned from previous experience, they were also equipped with tools helping them break into bunkers and hideouts. Freight cars were at the train station. Those captured were led there group after group.

"My grandfather on my mother's side had died in 1937; luckily for him. Now my grandmother Tova was taken when we were all captured. We were sitting in the arranged hiding place in grandmother's house. The hideout was three by three meters and the whole family, seven of us, was hiding there. Suddenly we heard the sound of the jackboots of the Ukrainian *Junkers* who went from one basement to the next in search of Jews. They banged on the door and found the hideout. When they opened the door we could see the sticks in their hands. We all almost fainted.

"Dad's effort to conceal the entrance was not a success. They gathered us near the synagogue and kept us for three days. My grandparents on my father's side had another bunker. It was also found and they were all removed from there.

"We all stood near the synagogue expecting a miracle to happen. People were ordered to hand over all their valuables. Everyone who was there gave up his things. But the quantity, when it was assessed by the Germans, was insufficient. Many people were beaten with a stick.

"I saw my grandmother remove a gold chain from her neck and put it in a bag in her hand. I didn't have time to think and wonder why the chain was still in my grandmother's possession. All our family had nothing to disclose after we'd sold nearly everything. It didn't even occur to me that the public place where we were concentrated could even offer a hiding place for the chain. It was not possible. Seeing my grandmother brought me back to reality. Grandma looked uncertain and was trembling. Grandpa asked softly if I was ready to receive the jewelry. He thought a young girl would certainly not be beaten.

"At the edge of the field, where we had been concentrated, there was an empty space. A big piece of linen had been laid out there. A German with a whip in his hand sat on it.

"I took the bag with the valuables from my grandmother and went to give it to him. Once I put the bag on the canvas where their loot was gathered I received a tremendous blow. It was very painful but I was glad it saved my grandmother from being hit.

"They put us in the trucks like cattle – worse, like sacks of potatoes, one top of the other. We were live human cargo loaded on trucks and taken to the train station."

"Luckily in those days the levers allowing the box trucks to tilt and pour their merchandise to the ground did not exist. Otherwise the Germans would have used them.

"At the station we were brought up to the freight rail full of people who had previously been brought there. We were herded into the train car with pushing and shouting. There were lots of people in each car. It was very crowded. The smell of chemical fumes brought stifling heat. It had been deliberately dispersed before they loaded the carriage with humans. It was after the war that I learned it was the same powder the Gestapo sprinkled to increase the stifling heat for their victims while in confinement.

"It was not possible to help those who fainted. People had no water to offer. Each person in the wagon was on the verge of fainting and made their best to stand as close as possible to the small opening along the wall near the roof of the wagon.

"The train stood for countless hours. People didn't know what to hope for. Would it go to an unknown place? Maybe the train would stay at the station a bit longer. Maybe soon an order would arrive to release us all."

Donia said that during all this time they were not given food or water.

Then the train began to move. The dense crowd in the cars tried to avoid stepping on those who had collapsed and were lying helplessly on the floor. This was almost impossible. Everyone was crying; hysterical. And some are still waiting for a last minute miracle.

Suddenly Donia realized she had not seen her grandmother who apparently collapsed and slid to the floor. She couldn't tolerate the situation and began crying hysterically too.

The train car had four openings that were windows of a sort. A number of young people bent the barbed wire that were closing these openings and apparently had jumped from the train.

Donia tried to talk to her parents and grandparents, persuading them to jump off the train or at least entice her sisters and brother to jump with her. But the adults and her siblings were afraid.

Donia made her decision. She said she was going to jump, no matter what.

"*Shpring my Kind, efszer dank dir wet blajben a Zichoren Von der Mishpoche.*" "Jump my child. Maybe, thanks to you, a memory of the family will remain."

Unknown hands picked her up in the darkness of the car and helped her get to the opening.

Donia was very thin. She managed to squeeze the upper part of her body out of the car. She managed to move in such a way that she could finally squeeze her legs out too. She held the opening lintel, trying to be as close to it as possible. She was ready to jump as a cat would jump on a prey. But the situation in which she was now was that of the prey trying to get out of the jaws of the Nazi beast.

The train reduced speed a little. Donia took the opportunity and jumped off.

Back to Stryj

Donia got back to her senses. Her father's last words were still ringing in her ears, "*Shpring my Kind, efszer dank dir wet blajben a Zichoren Von der Mishpoche.*" "Jump my child. Maybe thanks to you, a memory of the family will remain."

Donia had no clue if anyone else had jumped out of the train car or from other train cars after her.

It was dark when she regained consciousness. She didn't know how long she had been lying in that field. Her hands were scratched, swollen and covered in blood. She checked her limbs and found that no bones were broken and everything was more or less in order except for a pain in her jaw resulting from the loss of four of her teeth that had been knocked out when she jumped from the train. She had no clock or any idea of the date. She slowly regained consciousness and began to realize what had happened including the events of the three days and nights before her shattering jump.

The train with her entire family was gone. It was dark all around except for the pale glow of the moon. Donia rose to her feet and began walking in the opposite direction of the train's path. The walk was not easy. Her legs and hips hurt. She had no doubt she was covered with many bruises.

Donia occasionally sat on the ground. She had spasms of fear and doubt. What happened to her? Why did she jump alone leaving behind the family who should have jumped too? She should have stayed with them. Maybe they all went to work in Germany?

Donia had often heard that the Germans caught Poles and Ukrainians to work in Germany. Maybe this is why the Germans were recruiting Jews. Germany lacks working hands and decided to send this shipment of Jews to work in Germany.

But if people were to be assigned with work, why torture them before boarding them on trains? And why were they threatened and insulted and then tortured with those suffocating "treats" prepared inside the cars. And why did they take small children too? If people are sent to work, they don't need women and babies who are on the train. Were they also being sent to work in Germany?

These doubts were running through Donia's head. "If I'd stayed with them whatever happened to them would have happened to me." These were Donia's thoughts as she walked towards Stryj.

To her right Donia saw a field full of cabbages. She stopped, bent down and picked some cabbage leaves. They were wet. Donia used them to wash her face, legs and arms. The moon was bright but couldn't tell her if she had cleaned all the blood. She walked for three days.

When she reached Stryj, Donia went to where her cousins lived. She had not seen them in the train group. She found her uncle Joseph Heller, his wife Malka, her mother's sister, and their two children Meilech and Pepcia. This family lived three houses away from her house. They were hiding in another hideout that had not been discovered.

Uncle Joseph was about 43 years old. Before the war he lived in Truchanow, a village on the other side of the Stryj River. He was an animal dealer and was considered a fine professional. He could tell which cows would give milk and which cows were good for butchering. Joseph was familiar with the area and with the people living there.

Donia stayed with them. There was no point in going back home where everything was broken apart. Now, after the second big *aktion,* life was returning back to some sense of the new normalcy. Those who were still there believed, or wanted to believe, "This is it and there will be no more. *Moloch* got what he wanted. We have a chance to stay alive." This is what those who were waiting their turn were thinking. They were trying to interpret the events. They thought it was a crazy attack from the local commander. He was certainly drunk or did not receive the requested ransom.

Donia cried all the time. She asked herself and her cousins why she stayed alive. It was hard to describe the feelings assaulting her. All day long she sat crying, thinking how she had lost her whole family all at the same time. There were moments when she thought of taking her life. Her uncle made certain she didn't commit suicide.

The swelling of her injured body diminished slowly and after a month Donia was able to go back to work. She told her boss what had happened. He understood the explanation for her absence. She even perceived some sadness and pity on his face.

Donia went back to work as usual but the vegetable garden had been neglected during her absence.

Uncle Joseph understood the situation. He understood that they were doomed and there was no chance for any of them to survive. What his brother-in-law Matetyahu had said to Donia on the train was echoing in his ears as well. "Jump my child. Maybe, thanks to you, a trace of the family will remain." He had to do something for his brother-in-law so that his wish would come true.

Uncle Joseph took off his Star of David armband, came out of the ghetto and endangered himself by returning to his birthplace, the village of Truchanow. He turned to the village priest whom he had known since childhood.

The priest had become a friend of the Jews after an incident that occurred during the Soviet rule in the era between 1939 and 1941. The Russians had conducted searches for a Ukrainian Nationalist and asked that he be considered an outlaw. A local Jewish family gave him shelter. This act was engraved in the priest's heart. (This Jewish family saved the Ukrainian. The

Ukranian later joined the Gestapo and did not lift a finger to help them, and all the Jews of Truchanow. They all died after being sent to Stryj.)

The priest barely recognized Uncle Joseph. What a change since he last saw him three years ago. The Reverend remembering Joseph was very religious cautiously asked, "Would you care to eat something and drink a cup of tea with me?" Uncle Joseph, who had not eaten in more than a day, was very hungry and agreed, with no hesitation, to eat in the priest's home and even from his dishes. His survival had become more important to him than the *kosher* laws.

While Joseph was eating the priest told him he had gone underground during the Soviet rule because he heard priests were being sent to Siberia. Since the Germans had arrived, the priest never leaft the village as he did not want to see the terrible things happening to the Jews in the town. It was bad enough the villagers described it to him.

He was pleased that in his village none of the Jewish families were murdered. Unfortunately the Jewish families were forced to move to places of concentration in the towns. He'd arranged for the farmers with wagons and horses to drive to the place they had chosen. They did not meet the same fate as was heard of in other villages.

He didn't not know what happened to the Jews of Uncle Joseph's village and he hoped they were as healthy as Uncle Joseph standing in front of him.

The priest led his congregation on the same religious principles as in the past; love your neighbor. He was not forced to enter political issues. Recently the order was given to remind the faithful to keep their distance from the Jews.

Uncle Joseph said to the priest, "If a lot of people were like you, all these atrocities you hear about from villagers would not happen and I would not have experienced them first hand."

"Yes, yes, we are witnessing terrible times."

Uncle Joseph hearing what the priest was saying, asked if he could get Aryan papers for Donia, his sister's daughter.

The priest asked Uncle Joseph Donia's age. As Joseph told the priest, without hesitation the priest dug out a document bearing the name Efrozyna Skoblek and handed it to Uncle Joseph. He said, "This girl was the same age as your niece. She went into the forest to pick up mushrooms, slipped on a wet rock, tripped and fell into the abyss. She was killed. Her soul is now in heaven. These papers should save your niece."

Uncle Joseph returned the next day to the ghetto with authentic Aryan papers for Donia.

I asked Donia, "After you returned to the Stryj ghetto, did you report anything about jumping off the train to the Judenrat? How did you explain your sudden reappearance?"

"To the *Judenrat*?" asked Donia, surprised. "We avoided contact with them. These people lived patronizing us. They considered themselves "High Society." We were angry with them and avoided them if possible."

Donia continued to live with her uncle for a few more weeks. She went to work every day.

Flooding, Dilution, and the Final Liquidation of the Ghetto

In the summer of 1942 Jews from nearby towns were added in the Stryj ghetto in great numbers. These were Jews who did not work where they lived. Many of them came to Stryj on foot or in rented carts because Jews were not allowed to travel on trains. Those who tried were arrested immediately upon arrival. After a prolonged detention and selection, some were taken to the Hołobutów Forest where they were executed.

Most of the new arrivals were allowed into the ghetto. But some remained in custody pending further clarification. They were kept in terrible conditions for a long time. Finally they were also allowed to enter the ghetto which, at this stage, was well-guarded.

The workers who used to work outside the ghetto didn't know if they would be given the opportunity to continue working.

At the same time, some twenty miles away from Stryj, beyond the Carpathian Mountains in Hungary, Jews lead a normal life.

The Stryj Jews who had relatives across the border began to cross the mountains with the help of professional smugglers. The smugglers often robbed the runaways who then had to return, destitute, to the ghetto. There they starved to death or waited for the next *aktion* which would bring them to the Hołobutów Forest or the Bełżec death camp.

Individual escapees managed to reach their families in Hungary and, with their help, to the capital Budapest where most survived.

The Pikholtz family, before being sent to Bełżec, didn't try to cross the border into Hungary. Three cousins in Donia's family had tried their luck but were shot at the border. The Pikholtzes didn't want to dig a cave in the Carpathians fearing they would be found by the young anti-Semites and the informants who had dedicated themselves to looking for hidden Jews. It was believed that those who tried to escape and failed were instantly murdered. Why not give a chance to the Messiah?

There were other reasons to avoid hiding. Some adults were resigned to their fate and spoke calmly of the possibility of death. Some young people didn't want to leave the adults in their desperate condition.

The sayings, "What will happen to everyone, will happen to me," or "If you have to die, then die," was common in all towns including Stryj.

Everyone was looking for an option and a way to save himself and his family.

There were cases when Stryj Jews with no relatives in Hungary found smugglers to bring them over the border into Hungary. On the other side of the border in Hungary they found Jewish families and knocked on their door. They were generally met with hostility on the part of these local Jews. These Jews didn't want to hear about the atrocities taking place beyond the mountains. They demanded that these refugees, reduced to skeletons, went back to an inescapable death. They didn't even feed those unfortunates a piece of bread or give them a glass of water. They even wickedly threatened that if they didn't leave immediately they would call the police who would hand them over to the Gestapo.

Rumor had it that some Jews dug caves in the forests around the town of Skole. These caves were discovered by young Ukrainians who robbed the Jews in their hiding places and then handed them over to the Germans for a reward; a bottle of Vodka and a jar of molasses.

In February 1943, 1,500 Jews from the Stryj ghetto were executed in the Hołobutów Forest as a reprisal because they had captured a certain number of armed Jews who they accused of belonging to an organization of armed struggle.

In March 1943 the ghetto was surrounded by a special unit of *Sonder Dienst* (SD) and *Shupo,* the Ukrainian faction police and SS composed of former Soviet soldiers who had gone to the German side with their arms.

Adult Jews were dragged out of their homes and brought to the synagogue. Those who could not walk or showed some weakness or resistance were shot dead on the spot. The children, who were not under surveillance and were running aimlessly in the ghetto, were shot dead.

The Jews that were taken to the synagogue were left for several days without food or water. They were constantly abused and many died there. About 2,600 Jews were taken to the Hołobutów Forest and murdered.

3,500 remained. In April there were a number of small round ups. Almost every day Jews were assassinated in the town.

In May 1943 in the Hołobutów Forest 1,000 Jews were murdered.

In early June the ghetto was surrounded by special units of *Sonder Dienst* (SD), one unit from Stryj and another came from Drhobycz, *Szupo* (*Shutz* police) and Ukrainian police.

A few days before, the Jews who were allowed to live until then out of the ghetto in the Jewish quarter were ordered to enter the sealed ghetto. The ghetto was tightly closed and a thorough search was conducted. Houses were searched one after another and many of them were burned along with the people inside. They were burned alive.

Women and children were killed on the ghetto streets. Only

750 Jews were officially allowed to stay in the ghetto. 500 of them worked in the local sawmill and 250 in the glass factories.

Several hundred Jews managed to hide. They were constantly being looked for. Anyone discovered in hiding was immediately killed.

In July 1943 the glass industry workers were taken out of the factory and killed not far from their working place. No reference has been found of the fate of the 500 who worked at the saw mill.

At the end of July 1943 the final liquidation of the Stryj ghetto began. All the units, who had taken part in the previous *aktions* and many smaller liquidations, took part in the final liquidation. The operation was carried out under the supervision of *Obersturmfurher* Bock and *Obersturmfuhrer* Hildebrand.

All the Jews who were still in the ghetto buildings were gathered within the prison. Many were murdered while being transported to the detention center. A small group of Jews who possessed weapons showed they could defend themselves. 30 of the fighters were able to escape. 40 professionals were selected from the jail and sent to Drohobycz. The remaining were taken to the Hołobutów Forest and murdered there.

With the liquidation of the ghetto, the Nazis burned all the buildings. Employees of the *Judenrat* and the Jewish police were shot. Similar *aktions* were carried out simultaneously in nearby towns like Bolechów and Skole. Searches for hidden Jews were held almost every day. Every Jew that was found was shot.

Another chilling excerpt from the testimony of Jonah Friedler, Donia's uncle as it appears in the Book of Remembrance for Stryj: "It is the most dramatic night of my life; 19 July 1943. I felt the steps of the Angel of Death approaching the camp. My heart told me that I had only a few hours left. In the camp there was the atmosphere of an eve before an *aktion* which involved no morals and no laws. People drank and got drunk. Some hysterically laughed or cried to release the terrible tension that makes your head explode and squeeze your bowels.

"The two floors and the yard of the camp became a madhouse. In my neighbor's eyes I saw a bewildering and frightening reflection of myself. The nervous tension had reached its peak.

Soon everything would explode and I wondered how come it had not yet. Hundreds of innocent people in the prime time of their lives were oppressively enclosed in a filthy cage with a horrible stench. The last drop of blood was squeezed from us with hard labor for a piece of bread and a sip of water. After squeezing out our blood, they were now taking our soul. We are just waiting for their arrival which would surely come at any minute. Each of us saw them in our mind. Here come the Germans! They stormed in dressed in their green uniforms. They looked like wild boars. Here they were. They surrounded our camp. They placed us in a straight line so it looked orderly and legal. The orders were unparalleled, even before the death threat.

"We imagined that they led us through the streets of Stryj; through our streets straight to the cemetery. A man in his full youth with a strong desire to live was herded like a sheep to be slaughtered. He went to meet his fate on his own feet, straight to the mass grave. We pictured being forced to undress for the last time and remain naked. Then we were made to walk on a big board sort of like a trampoline that was placed over the hole. We made our last steps. I asked the Lord only one thing, my last wish, this was my last request. May the bullet enter my brain or heart. Allow this to be my end. In case I fell only wounded, I would probably not live. The dying would continue to fall into the mass grave until the heavy load of bodies would suffocate me.

"I suddenly woke up as if from a fever. My attention was brought to some tango music coming from just the other side of the ghetto fence. Just ten steps away there were fully lit rooms and festive, jubilant voices. People were laughing. The sound of people having fun reached me. I saw the dancing couples through the window. Those Ukrainian bastards were damn cheerful while in our windows the Angel of Death looked in. Thunder in the sky did not strike them. The earth did not open its mouth to swallow them. Cemetery pits were waiting to receive our bodies.

"I felt it was a crisis time that required a decision. Life or death! I tried to concentrate around that point. Whatever happened, we had nothing to lose. We must escape tonight. Tomorrow would be too late.

"My dear wife, who was always by my side during the struggle, stood by trembling, despairing and silent. She guessed my thoughts and the storm raging within me in those decisive moments. She also thought the end had come. We decided to leave the camp that very night. Exiting for an emergency was allowed for non-Jews only until 9 pm. The Jews were shot dead if they left the camp during the day. Only the echo of our footsteps stopped our breathing.

"When we got out of town and hid ourselves into an abandoned cow shed we were drenched in a cold sweat. We were soaked. It came through our clothes. I suppose such a sweat is experienced only once by someone. And this is when he is going to die. When his soul departs from his body. From that night until the Liberation on August 8, 1944 we had to face many dangers."

Stryj was declared *Judenfrei*, free of Jews. In honor of this a big celebration was organized by the civil authorities and local residents. The governor, Dr Hans Frank, was the guest of honor at the event.

Donia: the Young Girl Pretending to be a Non-Jew Named Efrozyna Skoblek

Donia worked in a tannery once owned by a Jew named Berger. This tannery was located in Nowy Świat about three kilometers from the center of Stryj. Donia continued to work as usual in the vegetable garden near the factory. The vegetables that she used to bring to her boss' wife in the past as well as secretly to her parents she now gave to her uncle.

At that time the situation in the ghetto was unbearable. In fact the authorities didn't provide any food and there was a great famine. The Jews who arrived at the Jewish hospital were instantly killed.

The employees could enter or exit the ghetto provided they had a certificate signed by the Gestapo. If one tried to leave the ghetto without a certificate it meant the death penalty.

Signs appeared stating: "Do not enter the ghetto." "Giving food or any help to the Jews will be considered an offense and will be punished by hanging." Christians were warned by posters written in bold letters and placed in eye catching places close to the ghetto and on walls around the city.

Jews with the letter W began to be organized in small camps near the factories where they worked. The Nazis used the empty houses of Jews who had been previously murdered for this purpose.

Regarding those selected "lucky" Jews, the Germans would sarcastically say, "They will survive the war." Every morning a Ukrainian policeman escorted the workers to their jobs. The officer was sent to prevent the mob along the way from taking advantage of the Jews or to explain to other authorities who needed them for other menial work. The officer often ignored his role.

After that period, only unproductive people who were not able to contribute to the German war effort were left in the ghetto. The plan was to gradually eliminate them.

The people knew it. Everyone was waiting for his turn in the hope he would be the last one killed. Everyone wanted to be the last one, hoping for some redemption brought by a sudden unexpected miracle: The Messiah. For these desperate people with no money, no Aryan friends and no luck, only the appearance of the Messiah could save them.

(Author's note: Can any human being imagine or understand the kind of thoughts an innocent person has, being locked in a cage like an animal who knows he will be killed one day and that only a miracle can save him. It is almost like a chicken that probably knows from the minute she breaks the shell of her egg that she will not die of old age.)

Cooking and baking were banned in the ghetto. Only one bakery supervised by the *Judenrat* baked bran (When you sift flour through a seive what remains is bran). This bran bread was obtained from the Nazis for the inmates of the ghetto. The ghetto had no electricity, no gas and no running water. Two hand pumps provided water for the residents.

Jews rose early and queued up to bring home a bucket or two of water. Everyone wanted to have some extra water supply at home. People had to be ready for an *aktion* to come. In order to be prepared for an *aktion*, people tried to stockpile water in their chosen hiding places.

A lot of small roundups by the Jewish militia were carried out on the orders of the Germans. The Germans used to set the quantity and the Jewish police had to provide the requirement or else. And everyone knew what that "or else" meant. Therefore the Jewish police continually looked for and found the hiding places of their fellow Jews. Sometimes they found their relatives among the fugitives. In those cases a dispute would come up which did not help the trustees, *Ordnungs Dienst*, the Jewish police, used to also deliver their relatives to be killed. Perhaps they thought that, thanks to their unwavering stand and dedicated work, the Germans would spare them.

Meeting with Rabbi Perlow

The Aryan papers Uncle Joseph arranged for Donia were not appreciated at all. Her mood was bad and her conscience gave her no rest. The thought that she had been selfish because she was the only one to have jumped from the train constantly plagued her. What right did she have to live? Maybe her parents and the rest of her family were in Germany and they were missing her.

Donia continued to work like a robot. Donia got up in the morning and went to the factory where she worked for several exhausting hours at the tannery. At noon she went to the garden. There the work was less difficult and she enjoyed it. While she was in the garden she had time to think. She thought she was living a horrible dream. She wanted to believe a miracle might happen and wake her from this nightmare; that the war, and all the atrocities, was only a figment of her active imagination.

Despite so many disappointments Donia continued to believe in the Almighty.

Donia had put the Aryan papers Uncle Joseph had arranged for her in a drawer and didn't think of using them. She became apathetic. She also clung to a fatalistic approach which was prevalent among those who didn't seek refuge in Hungary, just over the mountains, or those who didn't arrange for a secure hideout. These people, just like Donia, believed they had lasted so long due to good luck, fate and destiny or all three of these together. They believed that fate and destiny had looked after them so far and would continue to do so in the future. These people would say, "What destiny has in reserve for me will happen, even worse." "Whatever will happen to everyone, will happen to me." The most disastrous was, "If we have to die, then we die."

Uncle Joseph understood her state of mind and her wavering. He tried to persuade her to use the Aryan papers. He pointed out the facts and begged her to open her eyes.

Uncle Joseph turned to her and said, "Donia, look what's going on around us. People are dropping like flies. The Christians who have a soul and would help, are afraid to do so. The ghetto will be liquidated along with all the employees in the work places outside the ghetto. The Germans, with the help of their collaborators, have decided to eliminate the Jews of Europe. You have a chance to survive and see Hitler defeated. Damn him."

"I don't care what becomes of me," she answered apathetically.

Her uncle understood that without drastic action she wouldn't use the papers that he'd gotten for her at the risk of his own life. He said, "Because you hesitate leaving the ghetto as a Christian, we will go to the rabbi and ask his opinion. What the rabbi decides, you will have to abide by his wise decision."

The rabbi was none other than the famous Rabbi Shlomo Chaim Perlow, the former Chief Rabbi of the nearby town of Bolechów. Rabbi Shlomo Chaim Perlow was the only member of his family left after the first *aktion* in Bolechów in October 1941.

In the summer of 1942, following a German order, the rabbi with a number of his followers and all the non-working Jews in the Bolechów ghetto were moved to the Stryj ghetto. Being only a rabbi, his work was not considered productive and he was no longer necessary in the Bolechów ghetto according to the Germans. His place was in the Stryj ghetto.

Uncle Joseph and Donia visited Rabbi Perlow. Uncle Joseph turned to the rabbi and said, "Rabbi I come here with my niece.

She jumped off a train that was taking her family to the Bełżec death camp. Risking my life I arranged for her to obtain Aryan papers. But she doesn't want to use them. She was the only one to have jumped off the train and the only one in her immediate family to survive. We would like to hear the rabbi's opinion about whether she should use the Aryan papers to escape the ghetto and take this opportunity to survive."

Donia, an Orthodox teenager, dared not lift her eyes to look at the *rebbe's* face. (the Orthodox Jews way of speaking about a rabbi).

Donia heard the words of the rabbi, a knowledgeable and erudite person. She thought the rabbi himself was fighting with serious emotional problems and couldn't say anything dramatic.

The rabbi was very, very quiet. He looked tortured. He hesitated, took a little time to think and then said, "If by your words the girl has Aryan papers, she has an obligation to use them. She has to take the risk to get away from here and be saved. She has to do it. She has to survive."

After Donia heard the *rebbe,* her father's last words spoken before jumping the train car echoed in her head. She decided to take the risk.

(Author's note: It is strange that the rabbi thought the likelihood of staying alive was 50% and remaining in the ghetto waiting for death was 100% and yet it was still called a chance. Most Orthodox Jews were still waiting for a miracle. I told Donia that my sister had Aryan papers and a job with the priest in a small place not far from Lwów. The priest had arranged her papers. My sister was afraid to leave the house because about a week before the date set for her departure, her best friend was grabbed and, despite Aryan papers that were in her hands, she was not able to convince the authorities that her papers in her possession were genuine and they killed her. My mother was a follower of Rabbi Perlow, and always went to consult him about anything and everything. In this case of life and death, she did not consult with him and my sister was murdered.)

Rabbi Perlow after he had to shave his beard

With Aryan papers in her pocket, Donia kept on working at the tannery right up until the closing of the ghetto. At that time, in order to survive, people had to be vigilant, to hear and see everything.

After meeting the rabbi, Donia changed. She went back to her old behavior. She was a lively girl as in the past, listening and watching what was going on around her. A keen sense of awareness and precaution developed in every young Jew during the war. Donia's ears were therefore opened all the time in order to learn what was happening and what was expected of her.

One day Donia heard her boss talk with one of the employees. She learned that in the nearby town of Bolechów the Germans had just opened a casino. This piece of information was important for her. She had Aryan papers. One day she would have to make the decision to leave the ghetto and to make a move.

One Sunday, when she was working in the pigsty at the manager's house, Donia heard him speak again with his wife and a couple of friends about the German casino that was finally open in Bolechów. It was the second time she'd heard about it. Donia thought this was surely a sign. At that moment, she decided to rely on luck and find work at the casino.

Donia's mind was troubled. The distance between the towns

of Stryj and Bolechów was not great and there was a risk that someone would recognize her. But the risk of being discovered and murdered was much less likely than survival in the ghetto. She felt she had no other choice. She had to decide fast. It was several days before the closure of the ghetto

Donia thought, she had lived in the village of Synowódzko Niżne since childhood, but she hadn't been in Stryj that long. She had no Christian friends and had no established ties with them. Would anyone from her remote village come to the casino? It was almost impossible because the casino had the reputation of being patronized by Germans only. She decided that the risk of being recognized there was unlikely.

She needed to pay attention in all directions. She needed to keep her eyes and ears wide open.

In Synowódzko Nizne village and in the neighboring areas, where she was born, everyone spoke Ukrainian. From her early years she spoke Ukrainian with the housekeeper Nastunia who knew no other language as she was not Jewish. School teachers and their pupils spoke only Ukrainian and Polish. Ukrainian was spoken and Donia spoke it as fluently as a native speaker.

At that time Donia didn't know that Bolechów was considered the leather production center of Eastern Poland. This lack of information might have been part of her luck because otherwise she would have feared her boss the *Reichs Deutsche* whose manufactured leather could have shown up in Bolechów. As a *Reichs Deutsche* he could have exercised his right to enter the casino. But as stated, Donia didn't know that and it didn't occur to her.

Donia's decision took shape when she learned there was a plan to close the ghetto. This would prevent her from going back and forth to where her cousins were still living. Remembering Rabbi Perlow's recommendation the decision was easier. Donia's down-to-earth sensibilities warned her. Only by pretending did she have a chance to survive.

The night, before she left her uncles and her cousins, she cried. She prepared a bundle with the best clothes she still had and early in the morning she left the ghetto never to return.

Waitress at the German Casino of Bolechów

Donia decided it is now or never. She left her work. She went to look for a job outside of Stryj as a Ukrainian named Efrozyna Skoblek. Now she had to play her part outside of the ghetto. She didn't have time to rehearse. But the smuggling of animal skins which she's previously done in Lwów prepared her. She would perform beautifully.

Donia finished work in the garden early. She collected a number of cucumbers and tomatoes and put them in a bag next to her spare clothes. She also picked vegetables for the boss' wife. As usual she went to the factory manager's house to deliver the vegetables.

Before going away she'd decided to tell the wife of her boss that she was leaving them. That she was going to a distant cousin who lived in a village very near the Hungarian border. Here all the lies, the impersonation and the pretending started.

Donia told her boss's wife, "My aunt heard that I am here alone. She wants to look after me. Her Jewish husband, my mother's brother, was drafted into the Red Army at the beginning of 1940 and was sent to the front in Finland. She fears he might have been killed in the war and will never come home. They are a childless young couple. She has a farm with animals, cows and sheep and a fruit orchard. I will help her and I will feel at home."

"Go my child, our Ukrainian Lord will protect you because your Jewish God is not caring about you," the boss' wife said and she handed Donia a piece of bread to eat on the way.

Donia cried. She changed clothing in the toilet in the yard so she would look more Ukrainian. She removed the white band with the Star of David from her sleeve. She took the letter W off her coat's lapel and tore all the various permits and authorization papers attesting she was Jewish into tiny pieces. All these she threw into the toilet hole where she hoped they would rot forever.

At that moment two characters split and went different ways. That was the end of Dina Pickholtz for the moment. Efrozyna Skoblek was reborn in this backyard of the factory's manager's house. Donia wrapped her head in the traditional bandana,

Shalinowah Hustka. With her blue eyes and two braids she looked Ukrainian. She put herself in the hands of divine providence, fate, luck and destiny.

In the early afternoon, instead of walking to the ghetto, which the rumor said was closed and sealed; the very same day Donia started her new destiny.

Dressed as a Ukrainian villager and carrying a bundle of clothes and some vegetables, instead of going to the supposed aunt who lives on the Hungarian border, Donia went to Bolechów. The first step in being cautious was to avoid the Stryj main train station where she might be recognized. Donia walked to the first station, Slobodka, on the railway line from Stryj to Bolechów.

Donia went to the teller in order to buy a ticket to Bolechów. The cashier looked at her with attention. No doubt he saw this nice young passenger for the first time. Apparently the old devil enjoyed his chance of seeing this young girl stopping at his station. He gave her a ticket, taking more time than necessary.

"Maybe it was just me imagining he took his time. Maybe he suspected me and will contact the Germans," thought Donia.

Perhaps the old man would have started with questions such as, "Who are you and where are you from?" had it not been for the queue behind her.

Donia boarded the first train that arrived going toward Bolechów. Half an hour later the train reached Bolechów. She found herself facing a wide street. To its right there was an avenue of linden trees. The people who had just gotten off the train were heading there.

For the first time ever Donia was in this town, Bolechów. She didn't know the place at all. When she turned her head left and right she saw emptiness. She noticed that beyond the linden lined avenue there were several houses. The first one was two stories high. And at the far end of the street she noticed a large impressive building. Donia assumed the avenue was leading to the *rynek*, the town center.

Donia remembered hearing that the casino was near the Sukiel River. After a few hundred meters the linden lined avenue ended and it came to a junction where one could proceed right or left. Donia didn't know which direction to turn.

Here started her test. She would need to approach someone and ask, "Excuse me, where is the German casino?"

She was concerned that she might fail the first test even before she had a chance to get a job and create her character at the German casino. She would need to pretend 24 hours a day. She was now a Ukrainian villager.

She had to start acting according to her experience, the resourcefulness, the instinct, the courage and the luck necessary to play this dangerous game.

Donia recovered. She thought, "No doubt I am exaggerating. Less than an hour ago I went to the teller in the train station pretending to be a Ukrainian girl and bought a train ticket. It is true he scrutinized me for a long time. But had he been suspicious I would not be here right now. Surely I am overreacting.

"On the other hand, the man only saw my face through the teller's window. He couldn't see my body language which certainly indicated fear. Now I will have to stand right in front of someone and ask for directions. I hope he doesn't notice my fear. Will he become suspicious of me?"

Donia remembered when she pretended to be a student while taking skins to be sold in Lwów. Even then she had to play the part of an innocent girl going to school and not let the Russian detectives or police officers consider the possibility of who she really was.

But under the Russians Donia risked being arrested if caught. And, because she was a young girl, she would probably only get a reprimand. Now, in this unknown town under the Nazis, the game was much more serious.

Donia mustered all her courage and approached one of the older people who passed by.

"Praise Jesus," she said.

"Ever after," the man replied.

"Sir, forgive me. Where is the new German casino here in Bolechów?"

The man pointed and said, "I heard that on the other side of the big bridge, over the river, there is a new restaurant. That's probably the casino."

"Thank you sir," said Donia with a light smile and a significant easing of the heart.

It was her first challenge. Body language and the look on her face didn't betray her. Donia was encouraged. She didn't read any suspicion on the man's face. He simply thought she was a stranger, a Ukrainian girl from another town and nothing else.

Pleased with her first test she mustered up more courage and followed the direction the man had pointed. Donia walked along the main street holding her head high. She didn't know the town and no one knew her there. Thus began her acting, faultless and on her own.

She walked down Kosciuszko Street, the busiest street in Bolechów, crossed the bridge over the Młynowka Canal to the left. She could see a large flour mill not far from where she stood.

She hesitated for a moment. "Where is the big bridge? The man said I would find the casino after the big bridge over the river."

Instinctively she kept going. It had been only five minutes since, at the end of the linden lined avenue, the man had said, "After the big bridge over the river."

The channel she had just crossed didn't look like a river. She thought that the river here had to be about the size of the River Stryj. But that canal was just about five meters wide at most. She continued on, trying to look confident. Donia didn't notice that she was stepping on pavement recently created with tombstones from the Jewish cemetery.

When she reached the town square, the question arose whether to turn right or left. The street she was on so far crossed the square diagonally to the right. But there was also a sidewalk that cut through the left side of the square. She could see a street to the left.

Donia had to ask a passerby again. The question was what is the right direction to the German casino across the great bridge on the Sukiel River?

Again she used the same pattern as before. "Glory to Jesus," she said to the old passerby.

Once again she didn't notice any suspicion in the man's eyes and she didn't hesitate either.

Donia walked around the square and took Stryjska Street as per his instructions.

"If I continue on this street I shall wind up back in Stryj," she thought. After a few minutes Donia reached the bridge over the river. The river was not as large as the Stryj River. The bridge didn't impress her either. The bridge she crossed was much smaller than that on the Stryj River.

After crossing the bridge Donia looked to the right then to the left in search of the new restaurant or the German casino. She walked 150 meters without seeing any restaurant or store that might provide space for the casino.

What is this casino? How does it look? What do people do there? Is it a place like the casino in Monte Carlo, the name she heard of before the war where people gamble and play card games for money? She'd heard of people gambling huge amounts, which they lost, and then they committed suicide as a result. Is this casino like that one?

Donia slowed down. "The place is supposed to be somewhere here," she thought. "The first passerby said after the bridge. Here I am a short distance away from it. I have no choice than to ask a third person."

This time an older woman passed by."

Praise Jesus," Donia said.

"Ever after," answered the woman ready to continue on her way.

But Donia stopped her and asked, "Excuse me ma'am. I am told there is a new restaurant or German casino around here."

"It is there, beyond this street. Can you see a side street further up? The third house from the corner is the casino."

"Thank you and God bless you ma'am," said Donia thinking that she is probably fine as a Ukrainian. G_d bless Nastunia, the Ukrainian maid from whom she'd learned the Ukrainian customs as a child.

The experience of the three inquiries made her confident. Without a hint of awkwardness she entered the casino.

116

The German casino in Bolechów

"Praise Jesus," said Donia loudly as she entered the building.

"Ever after," said a young woman who was there.

"My name is Efrozyna. I am called Donia, my nickname. I would like to speak to the manager of this place."

"I run the casino," replied the young woman. What brings you here?" she added.

"Madam, I am seventeen and a half. I just left the orphanage where I've been since my parents died. I know household work perfectly well. I'm also good at gardening. I'm looking for a job. Would you hire me?"

The director of the casino replied without hesitation, "Yes, definitely. You are sent from heaven. We need help. We will hire you and give you a chance to prove yourself."

Donia remembered stories heard at home and at school that blamed the Jews for thinking of money and loving it too much. In order to keep this image of money loving as a Jewish habit she said, "Ma'am if you find me suitable to work for you, I ask if you will save my monthly salary; keep it for me. The savings will serve when I marry my friend Vaśko when he comes back from his work in Germany."

"It is quiet now as we have no guests for dinner in the casino. Even if we had, you would be free to organize yourself."

The director showed Donia her spacious attic room. "Here you have a clean bed and bedding. You will settle here and come downstairs for dinner. Tomorrow morning I will show you the work."

In the room there was a very large swastika and a big picture of Hitler hanging from the wall. This upset Donia. "I will try not to look at it. I have no alternative. I will have to get used to it," she thought.

After Donia organized herself, she went down to the lobby of the casino. The director took her to the kitchen. It was a large room and in one corner there was a big stove. It had a huge chimney built of red bricks. In it was a niche with a door for keeping dishes warm or drying mushrooms and sunflowers seeds. Near the chimney in the wall there was a large oven for baking. Next to the stove stood a huge cage made of iron in which the logs for the stove were kept.

On the opposite wall, on a low narrow wooden desk, stood a large water tank. Next to it there was a big vat to wash dishes. Under the table were enameled iron buckets. The third wall had a door in its middle and on both sides, two closets. The lower part of the closet was deep and tightly closed by doors. The upper part was less deep and featured two glass doors. Plates were arranged by size on these shelves. The fourth wall had a door leading to the yard.

Beneath the window stood a table and two chairs. In the middle of the kitchen stood a big table that had drawers on all sides. At the end of the table under the window a dinner was prepared for Donia. She ate with gusto. She felt especially hungry seeing that food was prepared for her. She had hardly eaten since the morning. Worrying about what would come next, she had forgotten about hunger.

In her clothes bundle there were several cucumbers and several tomatoes plus a large piece of bread. They were given to her by the manager's wife at the place where she used to work. What should she do with them?

She finished her hearty meal which was also exceptionally delicious. It was a long time since Donia had eaten such good food in such quantity.

The boss told her she would not be hungry while she was in

her employ. The casino got special benefits for the soldiers who pass by. They always have a lot of bread, sausage and eggs.

After she finished eating Donia asked if she could wash the plate, spoon and fork in the sink next to the wall.

"Of course," replied the manager. "Now is a good time to show you what must be done first thing in the morning."

The casino manager pointed to the buckets that stood under the work table and said, "Every morning you have to take the two buckets to the pump and fill them with water. Then fill the water tank with the tap and pipe located above the vat to wash the dishes. This water we use for drinking, making coffee or tea or cooking. Rinse the buckets before you fill them. The large container gets rinsed once a week. Now go to sleep because tomorrow you will have to do a lot of work. I'll tell you the rest of your duties tomorrow."

Donia went upstairs and made her bed. But before she lay down to sleep she thanked providence and fate that kept her safe so far and gave her the power to decide to proceed with hope.

Donia thought, "I just cannot go to bed right away. Maybe the director of the casino is behind the door listening, trying to find out if I am going to steal something or maybe to check if I am really a Ukrainian. If I am Ukrainian I must behave like one even when there is no one around. Why have I learned the Ukrainian prayers by heart? Is this not the right time for the test? I have to do everything possible to get through this terrible period. The *rebbe* said I had to choose whether to live or die. G_d bless the *rebbe* for giving me the courage. G_d forgive me for my temporary Ukrainian Christian belief."

Donia didn't know how to do it. Should she fall on her knees beside the bed and say the prayers? This Donia will not forget; she will have to find out.

Being alone in her room she sat on the bed and in a clear voice that could be heard beyond the door she said the Christian prayer,

"Our father who art in heaven,
Hallowed be Thy name. Thy kingdom come,

Thy will be done, on earth as it is in heaven.
Give us this day our daily bread,
And forgive us our trespasses,
As we forgive those who trespass against us.
Lead us not into temptation,
But deliver us from evil.
For thine is the kingdom,
And the power,
And the glory, forever.
Amen."

Donia was afraid to fall asleep. She worried she might scream in *Yiddish* during her sleep and the director, whose apartment is one floor below her room, might hear her.

Fatigue began to overcome her when some very loud snoring could be heard. The manager of the casino was fast asleep. Donia also fell asleep. She woke when the sun entered her room and a nearby rooster proclaimed the day had begun.

When Donia opened her eyes she didn't know where she was at first. She was not in the crowded room with her cousins. The pictures of Jesus hanging over the bed helped Donia remember where she was and all that had happened the day before.

She was concerned that the manager might have gotten up before her and was now outside her door and listening. Like last night, Donia lacked experience in Ukrainian behavior. It was not enough to know the language. It was not enough to pretend to dress like them. She also needed to know how to live among them.

Do I say the morning prayers only after washing my face and my hands, as is the Jewish custom, or right away when I wake up? Should I kneel down? Yes or no? She will have to find out.

Meanwhile, whatever the right answer Donia said her prayers again in a loud voice. Donia said,

"Heavenly Father,
Blessed be your name in heaven and on earth.

Give us our bread and forgive us our sins,
As we forgive our enemies.
Lead us on the path of honesty and good deeds.
That this is your greatness,
Strength and glory forever and ever.
Amen."

The first two words and the last one Donia said in a loud voice. If someone was listening they heard an Orthodox Ukrainian woman's voice.

She then looked out of the window. To her left she saw a large red brick building.

Donia cautiously opened the door. She didn't see the casino manager listening at the door from the other side. She was not there to listen if her new employee observed the Commandments of G_d.

It was dim in the staircase and everything was quiet in the casino. Donia left the door wide open so the bright sunny morning light lit the stairs. As she passed by the manager's door she stopped for a second, eavesdropping. She clearly heard loud snoring.

"I don't need her," thought Donia. "I'll start bringing in the water and then I'll light a fire in the kitchen stove."

Donia went to the kitchen which got its light from a big window. On the pegs next to a cabinet several aprons were hanging. Donia chose the one that was in the worst condition and put it on. She took buckets from under the work table with the water tank, opened the outside door and went outside.

Beyond the door there were a number of steps. And not far from them there was a pump just like the one they had in her village when she was a girl. Drinking water for the pupils at her school came from that water pump.

Parallel to the casino building, just eight meters away, stood a large hayloft and a small building attached to it. The small building looked like any of the toilets (outhouses) in her village, but it was bigger. "There must be more than one. Probably more than one person can use this at the same time," she thought.

Donia left the buckets at the pump and turned to the familiar little structure. Indeed these were two toilet spaces, quite spacious ones. Then she went around to the side of the outhouse and quickly peered into the barn. After checking out each building carefully Donia went back to the pump to wash her hands and face. The water was amazingly clean. She wiped her hands and face on her apron. Then she filled the buckets, brought them into the kitchen and poured the water into the big container. After another round trip to the pump, the container was filled. She was about to prepare the fire under the kitchen stove when the casino manager showed up.

There was no polite greeting of good morning or Praise Jesus. The manager turned to Donia and said, "Oh I see you know how a household works. I notice you've already filled the tank with water. It is true that you have to light a fire under the stove. But first you have to go to the dairy to get the milk products we've ordered. We order them a week in advance for the whole week's use.

"At the bottom of the cabinet there are pitchers. Take two of them; one for the milk and the other for the cream. Take out two of them and bring their lids too. Today there is also cheese to bring back from the dairy. So bring the blue enameled mold with its lid as well. Put them in your backpack. I'll show you the order list for this week."

Donia said, "There is no need to show me the list because I don't know how to read or write."

"All right then. Every evening I will show you what must be brought from the dairy," the casino manager concluded.

The director also showed Donia where the backpack was. Donia took the containers from the closet and put the cheese mold into the backpack. She wrapped her kerchief around her head and they both went to the front of the building. The casino manager showed her how to reach the dairy and explained what she should say when she arrived there.

Donia walked hesitantly toward her new challenge: the dairy. Once she found the building she saw drivers coming in and out with huge milk churns which they loaded onto their wagons.

People, jars in hand, exited through a side door of the building.

Donia went into the building and called out, "Glory to the Lord." A chorus of voices answered, "Forever." Behind the counter there was a young girl who asked, "Who are you?"

"My name is Efrozyna. You can call me Donia. I'm a new employee at the casino. The casino manager sent me here to bring back her order of milk and cheese."

The girl glanced at her notebook and requested the empty jars and cheese mold. Donia provided them and another girl immediately filled the jug with milk and the other with cream. She filled the mold with cheese and closed the lid.

Donia put the mold in the backpack, shouldered it and was about to leave when the girl behind the counter called out, "Hey. What's the hurry?"

A shudder ran through Donia and her soul almost left her body. Cold sweat immediately covered her back. What mistake did she make? Was she discovered? Was this the end? She gathered up her courage and asked, "What's the matter?"

"Nothing's the matter. There's no reason to panic. Don't you know you have to confirm receipt of these products by signing for what you've received?" asked the girl behind the counter.

Donia relaxed. "I'm sorry. The manager didn't tell me. And it wouldn't matter because I don't know how to read or write," she replied.

"No problem. Many people don't know how to read or write. Just dip your finger in this ink and make your mark or draw a cross." said the girl. She reached out to Donia with a long nail dipped into ink.

Donia drew a cross on the receipt and left the dairy. Outside she realized she shouldn't be so sensitive. She should be more confident, natural, and try not to falter over something so trivial.

It was only the day before that she started to play the role of an ordinary Ukrainian. She was supposed to be equal and as free as the other Ukrainians around her. She realized she would have to pull herself together if she was to survive. There was no room for her to feel inferior or timid. She had to learn to act like all the other people around her and not to worry so much. Her very survival depended on it.

Donia began working diligently at the casino. She washed the wooden floors of the three story building. She had to see that the three rooms intended for the Germans, only *Nur fur Deutsche*, were perfectly clean.

Recent Bolechów map

The German soldiers who came to the casino were mostly truck drivers on their way from Hungary or Romania. They drove fuel tankers or other cargo. They would stop at the casino, remain a couple of hours, eat, relax and then move on. Donia also had to clean the Great Hall where the local Poles and Ukrainians came twice a week to drink beer.

There was plenty of work. From morning to night Donia cleaned the tables and chairs, washed and dried the glasses, plates, and all the cutlery. She also helped prepare sandwiches when there was a large order.

The casino manager, a beautiful woman from the town of Stryj, was the widow of a colonel. She was left with two children. The current husband of the casino manager, Harasimov, served as a senior officer of the *SS* division *Waffen SS Haliczyna*, which consisted of Ukrainian Nationalists who hated Jews. Donia heard that this infamous division was trained in the town of Kraków. (Perhaps they were part of those who guarded the camps of Auchwitz-Birkenau which was close to Kraków. Their training consisted of tracking and murdering the Jews.)

When Officer Harasimov came to the casino he stayed with the casino manager in her second floor apartment. Donia didn't know if they were really married.

A month later he came home and stayed a week. The casino manager and her "husband" showed Donia that they appreciated her hard work and that she was diligent, working long hours every day without complaining. For Donia the work at the casino was much easier than that at the leather factory or in the home of the factory manager.

It soon became clear to Donia that the casino was located in the house of Dr. Goldszlag, a Jew who had been murdered by the Germans.

In order to keep possible suitors at bay, Donia took every opportunity to tell everyone she had a boyfriend Vaśko who volunteered to work in Germany and she was waiting for his return. Donia showed mail, supposedly from Vaśko, to the people who came to the casino. The locals believed that the letter came from her boyfriend in Germany.

They thought, "This educated friend knows how to read and write. He volunteered to work in Germany and took himself a pretty girl who doesn't know how to read and write when nobody else wanted to be involved with her."

Ukrainians and Poles in Eastern Poland believed that Jews were lazy and didn't want to do physical labor and were not able to do it. Jews tried to avoid serving in the military and refrained from any hard work that involved sweating. They thought Jews knew only how to trade and to earn money.

Donia, as a teenager, knew about these rumors and what the Christians thought of the Jews.

In order to blur her Jewish background even more, to remove any suspicion concerning her, Donia took another sophisticated step. Two months after she started working at the casino, despite the many tasks that were already on her shoulders, one day she turned to the casino manager with an offer that was difficult to refuse.

"Ma'am," she said, "We occasionally throw the leftovers into the rubbish. Why not take in a pig or two and raise them on the discarded food.

"Where will we keep the pigs?" the casino manager asked.

"I think there is enough room in the barn to build a pig pen," she replied.

The casino manager agreed. So a small pig sty was built in a corner of the barn.

A few days later the casino manager and Donia went to town to find out where they could buy small pigs.

At the municipality they were referred to the Municipal Agricultural Animal Institute where they could get two piglets for free provided one of them would be returned to the institute after its weight reached over 30 kilos. After returning the plump pig they could get another two for fattening. This is how pig raising started at the German casino in Bolechów.

Donia already had some training in raising pigs when she worked at the home of the leather factory boss. Donia knew the kind of food to be given to pigs and how to process leftovers that were suitable to feed the piglets. She knew how to raise them to become fat as quickly as possible.

Every two months Donia, the rural Ukrainian, could be found walking the streets of Bolechów with a fat hog. One of its hind legs was tied. The poor animal limped along behind her.

Donia returned to the casino with two tiny piglets ready for fattening. She put the screaming piglets into a bag which she hung over her back as she returned to the casino.

The Other Girl - Maryjka

East of the town of Sambor, in the Lwów district in the village of Kulczyce, lived a Jewish family named Last. They had two daughters. Once the family understood the dangerous situation, they obtained Aryan papers for their two daughters. The girls

126

looked like typical Ukrainians and could even speak a simple country Ukrainian. The parents understood that their daughters had a chance to be saved among people who could not read or write; a common phenomenon in the area.

If the daughters behaved like most Gentiles and forgot they knew to read and write, and remembered they could only speak Ukrainian, they could easily pass as Ukrainians and be saved. One of these supposed Ukrainian girls, whose first name is not known, left home to look for work.

Donia had been in the casino for several months by then and her work load had increased dramatically. Sometimes, around midnight, the casino manager would feel sorry for Donia and send her to bed.

"Do you want to fall asleep on your feet?" she would say. "If you don't go to sleep right now you won't be able to wake up tomorrow for a new day of work."

As if summoned, a girl showed up looking for work. The manager agreed to hire her. But the girl asked for time to make travel arrangements so she could go home to get her clothing. She promised that within a week to ten days she would come to work.

Two weeks later another girl showed up at the casino also looking for work. The casino manager was not in at the time. Donia invited the girl to sit and wait for her boss. Donia offered her a cup of tea. The girl introduced herself as Maryjka Kolczynski from a village close to Sambor. She said her father was very ill and her mother took care of him. She told Donia that in their area there was a huge flood causing major damage to their financial situation. She had to find work to help her family.

Although she seemed a real Ukrainian, Donia felt suspicious. The racial theory she had been taught, and which spread among the Germans, evidently had its effects on Donia too. There was a possibility that another Jewish girl might have had the same idea as Donia and came to work in the lion's den.

And after a second Donia said to herself, "If she is Jewish, Maryjka is no threat to me."

Donia told Maryjka about the other girl who was there two

weeks before and the job that had been promised to her. The other girl had promised to return a week to ten days later. The time had passed. Maybe she found a job that suited her more. So Donia invited the girl to wait until the manager returned.

"I will gladly suggest to the manager that she give you a chance. If you prove you are a good worker she will surely hire you. I think the casino manager will not feel obliged toward the other girl as she didn't show up as she had promised. If she shows up she will not be hired here."

When the casino manager arrived Donia presented the new girl. The manager accepted the idea and Maryjka started working with Donia. She started to worry that Maryjka might suspect her of being Jewish just as she suspected Maryjka of being Jewish.

Maryjka and Donia in Bolechów

Donia thought, "If I am wrong and she is a real Ukrainian, who knows, she may also be anti-Semitic. I will have to be very cautious."

In order to avoid as much suspicion as possible Donia took preventive measures.

The room they were supposed to share was relatively spacious. In the middle of the room there was a big chest. When the girls entered the room, Donia showed Maryjka that her mattress should go in the far corner of the room under the window on the other side of the chest. In this way Donia felt she could maintain the maximum separation for privacy. Donia thought that in doing so she also removed the risk of Maryjka's suspecting she was Jewish.

If, during their sleep, Donia uttered a word in *Yiddish,* the distance and the chest in the middle of the room would muffle the sound.

The girls got ready for bed and wished each other a good night. Donia, who was next to the switch, turned off the light. It was pitch dark in the room. Donia was sorry she switched off the light so fast before she could see if Maryjka was kneeling for saying her prayers.

"Maybe she is a non-believer or maybe she is Jewish as I suspect," she thought.

The room was quiet. "Is she awake? Or pretending to be asleep so she can check on my behavior. To be on the safe side, I will say my prayers and Maryjka cannot see if I am on my knees," Donia decided.

She sat on her bed and said in a loud whisper,

"Our father who art in heaven,
Hallowed be Thy name. Thy kingdom come,
Thy will be done, on earth as it is in heaven.
Give us this day our daily bread,
And forgive us our trespasses,
As we forgive those who trespass against us.
Lead us not into temptation,
But deliver us from evil.
For thine is the kingdom,
And the power,
And the glory, forever.
Amen."

For a long time Donia listened to hear if Maryjka was speaking *Yiddish* in her dreams. She wanted to know if Maryjka was also listening to her.

Two hours later, Donia realized Maryjka was asleep and allowed herself to fall asleep too. In the morning Donia woke up at dawn as usual and looked over to see if Maryjka had already woken up. She was surprised to see her standing by the window gazing out. A flash of fear ran through Donia's body. Who knows when she woke up? Maybe she heard something she was not supposed to hear? She started to prepare a good reliable explanation.

"Good morning," she said. "How did you sleep?"

"Well, thank you. But that damn rooster woke me up with his first call. I'll twist his neck if this continues. He will make a good soup. We will have to organize ourselves. We should bring up a bucket with clean water, a wash bowl and a spill pot. I woke up during the night. I was thirsty but too lazy to go down to the kitchen to get a drink. I didn't want to wake you. I noticed yesterday that the stairs squeak. If we had water up here we could wash ourselves and say our prayers here and not have to go downstairs. Yesterday you fell asleep without saying your prayers."

"Of course I said the prayer. But quietly, not as loudly and eagerly as you did."

"I was quiet at first. I thought you were already asleep and started to fall asleep myself when I woke up suddenly hearing you pray. It took me at least an hour until I fell asleep again," Maryjka explained.

"I fell asleep right away after saying my prayers," said Donia, adding, "Before the prayer I was thinking I should warn you before you fall asleep. I may shout out in my sleep in a mixture of languages."

"What do you mean a mixture of languages? And why do you shout during your sleep? Do you have bad dreams?" Maryjka asked.

"Yes, it's a long story. I'll tell you briefly, but only if you promise not to tell anybody," said Donia.

"I don't have anyone here I might tell. I promise I won't tell anyone *Bihme* (Ukrainian for a swear like G-d is my witness)."

"I am an orphan since a very early age. I think I was four or five when they put me in an orphanage. I don't remember exactly. I have no idea if I have sisters or brothers. Now that I am a grown

130

up I want to find out if they exist. After the war I might start looking for them. The orphanage was located in the middle of the homes of local residents. Some of the neighbors were Jewish children who spoke *Yiddish*.

"Among the Jewish neighbors was a nice woman who kept looking at the orphanage. One day she came up to the fence and asked me in broken Ukrainian if I would come to her home once in a while to play with her small daughter. She explained that she has to leave the house to go to work and her daughter was left alone. She added that I would get good food and good things plus a few *grosz* as pocket money. I told the woman I would love to but she had to contact the director of the orphanage to see if she would allow it.

"The orphanage director agreed and I went to the woman's house. When I came the first time the woman introduced herself as Fanny Freeling and the little girl's name was Ruth. They lived in Vienna, Austria until the Facists expelled them because they were born Jewish and were not Austrian citizens. Her husband Reuben was a lawyer and worked out of town. He left early in the morning and returned in the evening. She said the economic situation in Austria was better and she didn't have to work. Being deported they couldn't take everything and now she must help her husband support the family. She went three times a week to a large shop that sold everything relating to knitting. She was a knitting instructor there and had women clientele.

"I came to their house and ate lunch with them. For dessert we had a big piece of excellent chocolate. Then Mrs. Fanny explained to her daughter Ruth in their own language that she had to leave and that Ruth would stay with me. I would play with her. The girl agreed and we became friends very quickly.

"Mrs. Fanny left and we were alone in the apartment. The problem was that Ruth didn't speak Ukrainian at all. She spoke their language. Or maybe it was German. It was similar to what I hear people speaking in the casino. Ruth decided to teach me their language by pointing to objects in the house and telling me their names. I tried to remember these strange names. Iron was called *beagle eisen* and a key was *schlissel*. When Mrs. Fanny came home in the afternoon she gave us a glass of milk with a slice of bread and jam.

"Before I returned to the orphanage Mrs. Fanny gave me five *grosz*. Every once in a while I used that money to buy an ice cream from the seller who had his bike near the orphanage. Later on I found out that there were boys in the orphanage known as Gypsies who always managed to get money to spend. These Gypsy children also spoke another strange different language.

"I used to go to Mrs. Fanny's house two or three times a week to play with Ruth. I ate tasty food there and before I left I got the promised five *grosz*. At night when coming back to the orphanage I tried to remember the various words Ruthie taught me. I would fall asleep repeating the names and mumbling quietly, a rolling pin is a *walgeholc*, a breadboard a *lokshen breit*, a cutting tool is a *hack messer*, a water vase is a *waser krieg*.

"Sometimes at night the girls who slept in the same room next to me would wake me up and ask, "What are you babbling in that strange language?"

"I became used to this family and felt at home with them. I learned from them that the Jews are not allowed to eat pork and plates are separated for meat or dairy products. Their religion says that you must wash hands before every meal. I never saw the woman twist a chicken's head. She always took the chicken somewhere. Upon her return the chicken was slaughtered and plucked. On one particular holiday Mrs. Fanny served us a triangular cake filled with poppy seeds and nuts. On another holiday in the spring, they were not allowed to eat bread, so instead we ate a thin, flat disk as big as a plate. It didn't taste very good but it was interesting.

"On such holidays, Mrs. Fanny gave me a gift wrapped in colored paper. It was a sweater she knitted herself, a winter scarf or gloves. She used to attach a chocolate bar to it. Also on our holidays she would offer me a gift too.

"Our orphanage, apart from a small number of Gypsy children, was mostly Ukrainian. There were a number of Polish children too but there were no Jews. I was the only one child in our orphanage who knew and was familiar with a Jewish family and knew their customs. Other children didn't know anything about Jews except for what I told them.

"At the beginning of the war in 1939 the Soviets occupied our region. The authorities brought in several Jewish children as well as gypsy children from the surrounding villages. Our orphanage became international. The Russian commissar who came to visit us one day said that at orphanages in Russia there are children from 10 to 12 different nations and they all live together without problems. We Ukrainian kids made friends with the newcomers, small children of Jewish background as well as Gypsies. We were all good friends.

"The Russians organized trips for us to places we had never been. Life in the orphanage improved. Food was abundant; much more than before the war.

"I kept on visiting my little friend Ruth. The Freeling family was worried they might be sent to Siberia because they were refugees.

"Ruth's father, Reuben, was a nice man who spoke their language and some Ukrainian. He was quiet and gentle, and matched Mrs. Fanny' personality. They were a nice couple. Reuben didn't work away from home anymore. He started working as a bookkeeper in one of the town's factories. He offered to teach Ruth and me to play chess. When Reuben realized that I was not educated at all he taught me the games called Checkers and War.

"One day in the dining room of the orphanage a banner was hung with a Communist slogan, "He who does not work does not eat." Two commissars in uniforms came and explained that we children belonged to the nation. The young among us will become pioneers and the older *Komsomol* will have to go to work.

"The youngest were given red ties. A number of the older children were considered candidates to *Komsomol*. Several girls went to work at the textile factory in town. We learned how to use knitting and other machines.

"During this period, among all my friends there were three Jewish girls; 13 year old Ruthie, 13 year old Rozia, and 14 year old Miriam. They shared my room at the orphanage. They spoke *Yiddish* between themselves and to us they spoke Polish or broken Ukrainian. Every afternoon after work we would meet and discuss our day. We were a group of eight girls who kept a friendship. There were three Ukrainians girls, two Polish girls, and three Jewish girls. We were always together on weekend trips or any other occasion.

"One Sunday morning the town was suddenly bombed. One of the bombs hit the orphanage. One girl was killed and three other children were injured and taken to hospital. It was awful. There was blood everywhere. Broken bones, moans and screams filled the orphanage. I immediately ran to the Freeling's house to see Ruth. I was hysterical. I couldn't calm down. Mrs. Fanny gave me some valerian drops and after two hours I calmed down.

"I learned from Mrs. Fanny that her husband had heard on the radio that the war with Germany had started. Germany attacked the Soviets suddenly without any warning.

"When I got back to the orphanage in the late afternoon the place where the bomb fell was covered with sand. The blood stains were gone. We were told the injured children were not going to die. We were told not to visit them yet as they needed time to recover. An hour later we were told to stay together and not go to work the following day, a Monday, as we had to be prepared to be evacuated into Russia. Two days later we were still there and the Germans were in the town.

"The nuns continued to manage the orphanage. Two men with a truck and a driver showed up at the orphanage two days later. They went directly to the head nurse, Zofia, and demanded she gave them all the Jewish and Gypsy children. Zofia wanted to know where they were taking the children: after all they were orphans and had no family. One of the two men said, "These are not your issues. Your duty is properly raising the Christian children in the Christian faith. These are not Christian children.

"My friends were immediately and brutally loaded on the truck. We were not allowed to say good bye to them. This was a picture of evil and lack of sensitivity. We all sat down and cried. We didn't know what the future would bring."

Donia glanced at Maryjka and saw she was wiping tears from her eyes. "She has a soul," thought Donia before continuing.

"The food at the orphanage started to worsen and we started to feel the shortage. Two weeks later I missed my friend Ruth. I went to visit her. Mrs. Fanny opened the door. Her eyes were red from crying. The apartment looked changed. The curtains were drawn and though it was dark in the apartment I could see mess which was not the case two weeks before.

"Well you are here," said Mrs. Fanny. "Come in the other room and calm Ruthie please."

"What happened? Where have you been?"

"My husband Reuben was murdered," she said.

Ruth sat in the next room and was in tears. After I hugged her and kissed her I asked her to tell me what had happened to her dad. Meanwhile Mrs. Fanny joined us and apologized for not having anything to offer me. She had heard what I asked Ruthie and said, "Five days ago a German officer and a Ukrainian policeman stormed into the apartment. They turned everything upside down without a word. Anything of value they wrapped up. Then they ordered my husband to dress and follow them. According to the list Reuben had to come with them saying that after lunch or tomorrow he would be back. They gave Reuben the confiscated valuables to carry. The following day he was not back by the evening. I went to look for him at the police station. They beat me up for having the *chutzpah* (nerve) to interfere.

"He was sent out of town to work. When he is through with the work he will come back," they shouted at me. The day before yesterday we found out he was killed with 30 other educated Jews from the town.

"Mrs. Fanny explained to me that the Germans hated the Jews and that, in spite of both of them liking me, it was better if I stopped visiting them to avoid trouble for myself.

"I stopped going to them. A few months later I saw Ruth and Mrs. Fanny near the fence. We said hello only with a nod of the head. We didn't come close to each other. Ruth looked much older than her age, dressed in rags and she was very thin. They wore a white band with a blue star on their forearms.

"After several months I saw them again. Both were very thin but better dressed. Ruth was left to sit at a distance and Mrs.

Fanny, seeing that I was alone, came up to the fence. After saying hello she asked me to ask the director of the orphanage if she could talk with her.

"I went to the director and told her a Jewish woman requested to come over and talk with her. The director said I should take her to the fence. When the director arrived Mrs. Fanny turned to her said hello and introduced herself and said, "I have to ask a big favor. My husband was murdered almost immediately when the Germans entered town. I was lucky not to be caught in this *aktion* and have been lucky so far to save my child from starvation. Every day they collect between 15 and 20 Jewish bodies of people who starved to death. The Jewish council informed us that the authorities are going to move all the Jews that are not employed, and especially children, to ghettos in other cities. It seems that this is a death sentence for us. I have some savings I was able to put aside. I'll give you everything I have if you will take my only child and rescue her."

"The orphanage director looked at Mrs. Fanny and said, "Do you really think I would endangered myself and other children for a Jewish girl?"

"Without saying goodbye the director turned around and walked away from the fence. Mrs. Fanny froze. Tears ran down her face. She then said goodbye to me and walked away. I started crying. I had no idea how I could save that lovely little girl. Until that moment I didn't know what was happening to those people outside our orphanage. I wasn't happy with the director's response and I wondered if my friends Rozia and Miriam were still alive. They were taken in the very early days of the German occupation. They didn't have any family. Who could help them survive? I went up to my room, packed my things, and ran away from the orphanage. Two days later I was here."

Maryjka sat on her bed wiping her eyes.

"Yes, Maryjka hard times are coming to the world and we cannot help. I know this was a long story but I want you to understand if you hear me calling out in a foreign language during my sleep. It's only due to the experiences I've had and the traumas that go along with them."

Maryjka responded, "I fortunately, in my village, didn't see or go through such horrible things as you've described. A number of Jewish families lived in our village. I didn't have friends among them. One day they were ordered to move to the town of Sambor ghetto. What happened after that, I don't know."

After this long conversation, both girls were emotionally drained and ready to move on to other topics.

"It seems to me I heard you pray last night," said Maryjka.

"I pray, but sometimes I forget to," responded Donia.

"Let's go downstairs and start our jobs," suggested Maryjka who was two years older than Donia.

Donia's spirit was good. She felt proud of herself for being able to tell such a story. Also Maryjka's comments made her feel good. The way she reacted led Donia to believe she wasn't in any danger from Maryjka. "Still," she thought. "I should check one more time and be cautious."

For the next several nights Donia said her prayers and fell asleep only after she was sure Maryjka was fast asleep. After Donia's confession to Maryjka the latter didn't volunteer any further details about her life. The girls didn't exchange any news such as what's doing at home? How is your father? What are the living condition after the big flood? Are you homesick? How come your friend isn't sending a photo? All these things are usually asked between girls working together. Donia didn't want to embarrass Maryjka suspecting she was Jewish too. Maryjka didn't ask questions either such as where exactly are you from? Despite the fact that they worked under the same roof and slept in the same room, they kept a lot of their personal histories to themselves and didn't pry into the other's past.

Donia worried, "How can I avoid speaking while sleeping at a time when vivid memories are running in my head? How can I block images, emotions and feelings coming in waves into my subconscious when all around me is so terrible? How is it possible not to think about one's mother, father, grandfather or grandmother, siblings, uncles and cousins who were very recently killed? How can anyone digest all this without nightmares?"

Donia was frightened of her own thoughts. "Quiet," she

reminded herself constantly with great strength. There was only one answer and that was to keep silent. Speaking would only be necessary during her work for the casino manager.

As a daily routine she scrubbed the floor, brought in the milk products and fed the pigs. But this was not enough to keep her from thinking about the past. She tried to minimize her thoughts and memories from home.

Donia recognized the necessity to really become Efrozyna Skoblek. She needed to adapt her personality in order to replace Dina, the daughter of Mathias and Yocheved. Efrozyna Skoblek didn't need to fear the Germans or the Ukrainians around her. But Donia had a right to tremble with fear at the first cackle.

Donia realized the power of Efrozyna Skoblek. It was not only a fake document. It was the only thing that would keep Donia alive. Donia remembered a verse of the Proverbs, "Life and death are in the tongue." She knew that she had to BE Efrozyna and that the Jewish girl named Dina must disappear.

Donia's instinct, even at 17 1/2, told her that Maryjka should get used to the fact that Efrozyna was a hard-working, religious and conservative girl who wasn't much for conversation. If she succeeded in getting Maryjka used to her quietness it would considerably diminish Donia's fear.

In normal circumstances, if a person tried to change his/her identity and acted differently, that person would face great difficulties keeping the charade up for long unless he was professionally trained. What enabled Donia to adopt the character of Efrozyna was the lurking Angel of Death. There was no better teacher.

A person who loses all of her dear ones knows he/she can be dead any minute. In such a situation two things can happen. This person becomes hyper alert or he/she could become ready to flirt with danger because he/she knows they have survived thanks to luck or fate and what he/she does is not really relevant.

Donia repeated several times that, after what happened to her family, she stopped appreciating the value of her own personal life and some part in her didn't expect to survive.

(Authors remark: Many of those who survived asked

themselves for many years "Why me?" It is not an emotional question but an existential one to wonder why your siblings have been taken away to die and you stayed alive. There are no logical answer that can be explained by certain moves or actions. Donia jumped off the train which most certainly was carrying her and her family to death. She could have been more injured. She could have been turned over to the Germans. But none of this happened. She survived if only because of luck and fate. Her life was threatened all the time. But because of what happened to her family, Donia wasn't afraid of death. It was an out of the ordinary state of mind that over time allowed her transformation from Dina to Efrozyna. She learned to trust in her ability to live like Efrozyna in her looks, her countryside clothes and in the scarf she used as a wrap. These things were important to her.)

Donia noticed that the casino manager avoided giving Maryjka the real heavy work such as scrubbing the wooden floors. It was hard work that only Donia could manage besides the other chores. Maryjka was not a particularly hard working girl and the casino director noticed it.

Donia scrubbed the floor with wet cloths she wrapped around her feet. She moved them quickly, small steps at a time until the floor was shiny. It wasn't fair not to divide the work equally. But it was a big plus for Donia. Hard work, conscientiousness and dedication made Donia trustworthy in the eyes of the manager who left her to her own devices for a long time during the day.

Donia knew well that every hour that went by quietly and without unnecessary contact with people was an asset. In the evening when the girls went to bed they showed no interest in each other as the suspicion was mutual.

Donia's natural fitting into the role of a simple Ukrainian girl made her see the casino as her security fortress. She tried not to go outside the courtyard of the casino despite her self-confidence and because of it in fact. Each step was calculated. Self-confidence could make her loose her sense of security. She was used to working. It was becoming routine. She didn't need extra hindsight to check if someone recognized her, suspected her or followed her.

The walk to the dairy worried her every day. Maybe on the way she would meet a Jew hunter who might want to explore whether she was a genuine Ukrainian who stood in front of him or a Jewish girl pretending to be a Ukrainian.

As long as Maryjka was not there she had to do this dangerous mission.

Maryjka's behavior was more Ukrainian than hers. Maryjka was not afraid to visit with the neighbors over the fence from time to time, so Donia gently passed on the task of walking to the dairy

In order to further describe Maryjka's Ukrainian mentality Donia told me the following story: "Once Maryjka was sick. Without checking her fever or seeing a doctor she went to a Ukrainian neighbor who rubbed oil on her back and put her on the *pripetz'ik*, (a flat space above the stove). After two days Maryjka came back completely cured."

On Sundays they used to go to church during the two hours the casino manager allotted to them.

About two months before Maryjka came to work, the casino manager decided she needed a bookkeeper. She turned to a friend in town asking if he knew anyone among the still living Jews who was a bookkeeper to help her at the casino. The man knew Shlomo (Siumek) Rainhartz from when Siumek was a bookkeeper at the bakery formerly belonging to a German named Shlamp. Her friend recommended Siumek.

The casino manager asked Mayor Hucalo for permission to use Siumek. The casino and the forced labor of the leather industry were under the responsibility of this bastard Mr. Hucalo. The manager of the casino asked him to send her the Jew Siumek Rainhartz who some close friends had recommended. He said there was no problem. He would send her the Jewish bookkeeper.

At that time there were still three forced labor camps in Bolechów where Jews who were useful as the Germans called them (*Nutzliche Juden*), still lived. One such camp was near the barrel factory. (The author of this book was one of the Jews working there.)

Another camp had been organized at the largest sawmill. There was also a camp for the leather industry workers.

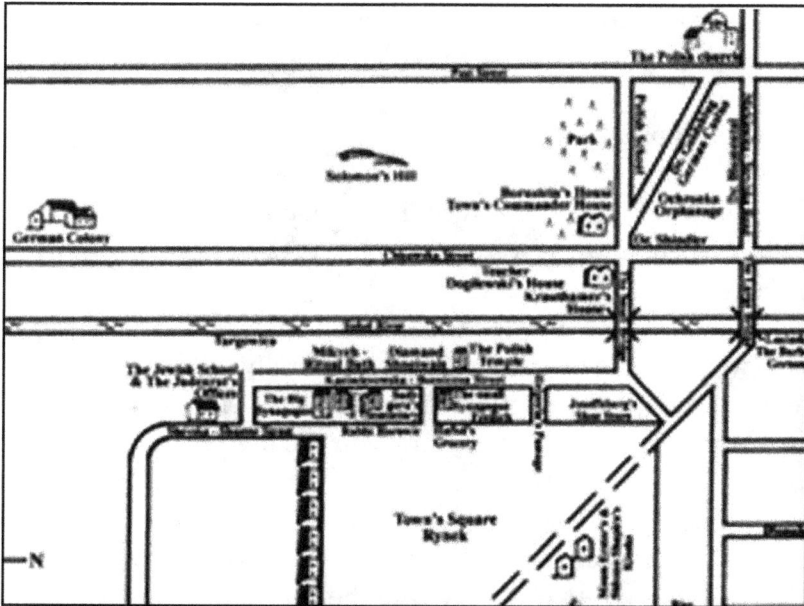

Part of Bolechów map according to the writers' memory - where Donia's activites were performed

Mayor Hucalo sent the Jew Siumek Rainhartz who worked in the leather factory once owned by a Jew named Kurtzer. During the Nazi occupation this factory was owned by the Consolidated Industrial Urban Plants.

Shlomo (Siumek) Rainhartz was born in Bolechów. He and his family lived on the main street named after the famous Polish poet Adam Mickiewicz. On one side of their modest home the well-known Dr Blumental, a famous doctor among the past doctors in Bolechów, lived. One of the most beautiful streets in town was named after him even though he was Jewish. On the other side of the house there was a small synagogue called in *Yiddish die Kapliczke.* (In Polish *Kapliczka* is a chapel in the woods or at a crossroad where Christians could pray when they pass by.) This synagogue, which was off the main road, was always open and Jews passing by would come there to pray.

Several years before the war Siumek established a good private library. He lent books to the citizens of Bolechów. People from the town could come and chose the book they wanted to read. Siumek's library became the meeting point for Bolechów's intellectuals.

When Siumek noticed that people came to him every day and even more toward the end of the week, he bought a franchise for the sale of National Lottery tickets. Up to that time only the few who visited Lwów were able to buy lottery tickets.

Here in this remote town it became an attraction. Luck helped people win as much as million *złotys*. There were not many winners and the amounts were generally small. But, as sales grew, winnings became more frequent. Just before the outbreak of war one of Siumek's customers won the big prize of a million *złotys*. He was Israel Adler, the author's uncle.

During the Soviet regime, from 1939 to 1941, Siumek's library was nationalized. He got a job as a bookkeeper at the local German bakery. At this very time he married Malka Walik, a beautiful blond with long braids.

At the beginning of the German occupation, when Jews were still living in their own apartments, Siumek kept working at the bakery named Shlamp after its German founders. His work there entitled him to get one loaf of bread every week in addition to the *Judenrat* ration. Malka went to the bakery once a week to get the loaf of bread. This loaf of bread was shared with Siumek's parents.

One day, after cutting the bread, she took the piece for Siumek's parents and headed toward their home. After passing the big bridge, coming close to her in-law's house, the notorious Ukrainian policeman Matwyjecki stopped her. After he found what she was carrying he ordered her to follow him.

The Ukrainian neighbors of her in-laws observed the scene from the window of their house. They came out to convince Matwyjecki to leave Malka alone and he did.

All the family members of the young couple were murdered in different actions. Malka and Siumek were lucky. They were among the few still alive in the summer of 1943. They were hoping that the protection of the letter W would increase their longevity as long as they worked in a leather factory.

Malka's sister and her husband worked in one of these labor camps. They also had the talisman letter W.

Siumek was given the job of bookkeeper at the casino. Once a week he went to the casino to get the paperwork to do the business accounts. Upon arrival Siumek was offered a glass of hot tea and a sandwich. He saved half of his sandwich to share with his wife. After he finished drinking the tea he would get the books and the receipts of payment made during the week from the casino manager.

When Siumek was leaving the casino, the manager would say in Ukrainian "*Takoj fajnyj Żydok szkoda szczob takogo ubyły.*" ("Such a nice Jew. What a pity to kill one like him.") This is what she said but she didn't lift a finger to rescue him. The girls heard her say it several times.

One day an *aktion* broke out in the Jewish labor camps. All the Jews fled to the fields and the forests. Even Siumek and Malka ran to the forests on the Carpathian slopes. Malka's sister and her husband also fled.

The *aktion* ended after two days. The Germans didn't succeed in this *aktion*. They caught around 60 and murdered some 80 Jews.

People had to choose between a courageous decision or hesitation, which would cause them to pay with their lives.

All sorts of people would show up at the casino. There was a man who worked at the German barrel factory, the *fass fabric*. Donia doesn't remember his name. He always joked when ordering something. When the waitress said, "I shall serve you immediately sir," he would reply in Polish "*Teraz zaraz, czy zaraz potem.*" "Right away or soon after." He had learned a few words in Polish and was proud of his ability to acquire the language, but his intention was to get fast service. This German came every week, mainly to drink beer.

"He had a very German name but I can't remember what it was," Donia said.

Donia didn't make any contact with Jews at the labor camp. She knew of the existence of these camps but didn't ever see them. The only Jew she saw every week was Siumek. But despite knowing he was Jewish Donia couldn't show him any signs of friendliness, even when she filled his cup of tea or made a sandwich for him. She was even afraid to add an extra piece of sausage to his sandwich, fearing it would arouse suspicion of her sympathy toward the Jew.

She knew she should not show interest in what was happening to the Jews. This issue did not interest any of the casino visitors and was not even a subject of conversation between local Poles or Ukrainians. They didn't care what was happening to their Jewish neighbors. The casino patrons who came twice a week for a beer never mentioned the Jewish people who had lived among them for generations. No one ever mentioned the owner of the house, the famous Jewish doctor, who used to own the building where the casino was now located. For them the Jews were like a flock of geese or chickens sent to be slaughtered or those who were waiting for their turn. Nobody makes a case for the flock of birds in the chicken coop.

One time, in the winter 1942 /43, Donia saw the policeman Piatke, that son of a bitch, with his frighteningly menacing dog next to him, leading a Jew in rags, walking to his death barefoot on frozen snow. Donia saw this sight another time as Piatke lead other Jews to their death.

What Donia saw made her fear this man, particularly since he often patronized the casino. When Piatke entered the casino, if there was no one else to serve him, she was obliged to give him a cup of tea or a beer of his choice. Donia would serve him and then would move away from his seat without stopping next to him. There were rumors that his dog was trained to discover Jews. This frightening dog lay at his feet at all times.

Officer Piatke was tall and thin with brown hair. He was about 40 years old and was quiet. He was of Czech origin but it did not disturb him to speak fluent Ukrainian. Sometimes, when Donia had no choice, she spoke to him in Ukrainian in spite being scared to death of him and his fearsome dog.

Donia had to remember not to show that she could speak languages or understand them. She should not come out with one word of Polish. She could not show signs of fear. She worried that Piatke might notice, suspect her and discover her true identity. Piatke had been appointed by the Germans as a supervisor of the town of Bolechów.

(Piatke disappeared two weeks before all the Germans fled the area in 1944. He must have had insider information and knew to leave before all the other Germans.)

Donia doesn't remember the names of the Ukrainian police officers or Germans who used to come to the casino. She played the role of a simple Ukrainian girl who was illiterate. It was to her advantage.

When I visited Donia to hear her story, I showed her pictures of the house that was next to the casino, and pictures of Eugene Matwyjecki and his wife Daria. He was once of the greatest killers in Bolechów during the Holocaust.

Donia doesn't remember the house or the man. Was this her protective instinct? Suddenly she was a simple, illiterate Ukrainian girl who knew nothing. After about a minute Donia added, "Then he was in uniform. I don't recognize him today after so many years wearing civilian clothes."

Once, Donia almost forgot who she was supposed to be. A priest who occasionally passed through Bolechów came to the casino. He was a friend of the casino manager's former husband. The director's first husband wanted to become a priest at one point in his life and this is how they met.

The casino manager was not home and Donia was busy washing the floor. Donia stopped what she was doing, wiped her hands on the apron as always and invited him to sit in the important room meant for the Germans since he was an important person. She offered him a cup of tea.

The priest began to ask her who she was and where she came from. Suddenly he said, "You have a very rich Ukrainian vocabulary and you speak without errors. Where did a country girl learn to speak so well?"

She didn't feel afraid and replied, "I learned a lot from the casino manager. I learned words from her that a simple girl like me never heard before. I wouldn't be able to use them if I didn't hear them from her."

"There's no doubt you should be grateful that the manager speaks Ukrainian to you," replied the priest. He was satisfied that his friend's wife not only gave work to a poor orphan but also provided her with a rich vocabulary.

Donia didn't sleep well at night. She feared the people around her including Maryjka. She'd learned about the Jews in the camps. Siumek used to come every week to collect the paper work and she saw how afraid of everything he was.

Several months before Donia heard how the Germans were defeated at Stalingrad and suffered in Russia. Rumors were circulating about the uprising of the Warsaw ghetto.

She thought, "Maybe Germany will fall and the Germans will withdraw back into Germany. But before it happens they will kill all the Jews within reach."

Qualms of guilt harassed her. Donia felt that, since she was alive, she must do something; take some action.

Her entire family had been murdered; her parents, sisters, brothers, grandparents. In case she was murdered the whole world would not know there was a girl named Dina Pikholtz. No one would mourn her. Her life hung on a thin thread. She had nothing to lose. In order to silence the pangs of sorrow and guilt she was feeling she decided that she should do something useful with her life.

As a young Ultra-Orthodox girl until very recently, Dina probably subconsciously believed her parents and providence would see her good deeds and forgive her for jumping off the train alone, surviving and pretending to be a Christian who went to church, which is absolutely forbidden according to the Jewish tradition. Her Jewish ancestors, when thrown out of Spain, sacrificed their lives and refused to convert. And she, Dina, who recently sought the advice of a rabbi about whether or not to use false documents, was regularly going to church. "God forgives those miserable hands who raise pigs," she thought.

She decided that she would have to save the Jew who does

the accounts. This would be her compensation for her chance of survival. If I survive I may be able to save someone else. This will be my penance for the sin of being alive.

She did not remember the words of the *rebbe* who said affliction would be brought to an Orthodox girl who ignored or did not remember the tenets of the Jewish religion that life is the greatest commandment. Life is definitely not a sin. The desire to stay alive cannot be considered an offense.

Donia was thinking about this when she mentioned to the bookkeeper her intention to hide him. Siumek probably didn't understand it either. Probably he didn't believe her or, even worse, trust her. He insisted that he had a wife and wouldn't go into hiding without her.

Donia decided to share her plan with Maryjka as she always suspected her of being Jewish. To check on her suspicion in a tangible way she decided to test her. Better that Maryjka shares the responsibility of hiding this couple she'd chosen to save.

Donia tried to recruit Maryjka in her plan regarding the young Jewish bookkeeper of the casino. She said, "You see the Jewish bookkeeper who comes here every week? He is married but has no children yet. Don't you think it's a shame the Germans will murder them? How about looking for a hideout for them?"

"Do you know what the risk is for hiding Jews?" asked Maryjka.

"Yes I know. But I've started to feel sorry for this man. I thought, if you agree to a cover up, together we might save them both."

"And where do you think we could hide them?" This question on Maryjka's part was a good sign for Donia. Maryjka didn't refuse or reject the idea right away.

Donia noticed there was an expression of grief on Maryjka's face when she mentioned the murdering of the Jews and some concern when she started to talk about where to hide them.

Donia decided to talk to Maryjka without revealing everything. She explained, "There's a lot of hay in the barn. They could hide there temporarily. A better place would be the attic above the two toilets in the outhouse adjacent to the barn."

Bolechów: Entering from north

They will have to move two or three boards, enter and return the boards back into place.

The girls agreed to prepare the hideout over the two toilet cubicles of the outhouse. One day they would offer the couple that spot to hide.

The next time Siumek came to get the paperwork the manager wasn't there. The girls invited him in for a cup of tea. They asked him where he was working and where his camp was located.

"Can we come and talk to you and your wife at the camp?" they asked.

Siumek told them he was working at the leather factory. On Sunday they could come close to the gate of the camp. He and his wife would be waiting for them. They would approach when they saw them.

"In two weeks we have to prepare a lot of food, many sandwiches and soup," the casino manager said. Our guests will come for lunch or in the afternoon.

Donia thought something bad was brewing. She was worried. How come many Germans are coming here? What for? Usually there were two or three Germans sitting in a room reading the

148

newspaper or on the restaurant side drinking beer. But if the Germans are so numerous, and there are still Jews in the labor camps, they surely are coming to eliminate them.

Donia's intuition made her remember that the Stryj Ghetto had been terminated long ago. There was no doubt that the Germans had since eliminated the small camps near the workplaces. Now they will kill the remaining Jews in the town of Bolechów. She needed to act quickly.

Donia requested that Maryjka be the one to ask to provide help for the young couple. She did it to win Maryjka's trust and also to show respect to her since she was two years older. It was also an effort to cool down Maryjka's impulsive nature. Donia thought that if Maryjka assumed some of the responsibility for the risk, it would moderate her behavior for the better, to calm her.

The girls prepared hay near the passage to the attic of the outhouse. They brought two big bags that Malka and Siumek would fill with straw to make mattresses.

On Sunday the girls took advantage of the two hours allotted for worship and rest. Wrapped in their traditional Ukrainian scarves, the girls went to the Cerkiew in Bolechów's town square. Then they turned towards the leather factory labor camp that once belonged to the Jew Kurtzer.

The camp gate was wide open and the girls noticed Siumek and a young woman who stood not far from the entrance to the camp.

The girls came closer, Siumek introduced Malka, his wife. The girls asked why they stood at the fence since the gate was wide open. Siumek explained that they were not allowed to leave unless they were going to work. He told them that this camp was temporary and within a few days they would be moved to another camp across town.

After they got the explanation about the camp, without any preliminaries, Maryjka started to talk as usual without manners. The Ukrainian girl said, "*My Choczemo was schovaty.*" "We want to hide you."

It was a miracle coming true. Siumek did not believe he had

a chance to survive. He also had not told Malka about Donia's premonitions, not being certain of the seriousness of the young girl. Why disappoint his young wife if it did not lead anywhere. Just three weeks ago they were a step away from death when bullets whistled, passing close by while they ran in the woods and the fields.

So far they hadn't gone into hiding because they had no money to pay for food - definitely a necessity. They has no money to pay their rescuers as was the custom.

The rescuers took advantage of the *aktion* when the Germans wanted to eliminate all the labor camps in which there were Jews. Most Jews managed to escape to the fields and the woods. Everyone stayed there for two days while the *aktion* was raging. (The author of A Jew Again had the same experience at the very same time)

A new camp was under construction and they were going to be relocated there. This would be a real camp with three rows of fencing and watch towers which were being built. It was difficult to believe the new German commander when he said this is for their own good and that it was to protect them

Three weeks ago he picked them up in a meadow next to the sawmill and proclaimed in the name of the Fuhrer that he would not harm the Jews. He built a new camp with eight or nine barracks. How does he expect to accommodate over a thousand of Jews, some of whom are married? How does it fit the Fuhrer's orders not to harm Jews? How can he accommodate more than one thousand Jews in eight large sheds? Whatever the size of the shed, they would have to squeeze about 140 people into each. Where are the nurseries, school for children or places for adults as he promised? There was a hospital at the Ruski Bolechów. Would it still exist in the future?

The girl's offer to hide Siumek and Malka seemed too good to be true. It must be a trap. But what could be done? Everyone was in a bad financial situation. And here these non-Jews were ready to hide Siumek and Malka even though they had no money.

"No way. They want to take what is left and turn us in to the Germans," thought Siumek.

"We are not one hundred percent confident our plan will succeed but we know they will kill you very soon if you don't go into hiding," said Donia seeing some hesitation on Siumek's face.

"We know that a lot of food was ordered to be ready for next week. The last time this happened it involved atrocities and murders. The damned policeman and killer Piatke came with his dog."

Donia didn't know about the German participation about a month ago to eliminate the last Jews remaining in Bolechów. The roundup failed because only 80 Jews were killed out of a thousand who were still in the camps.

The girls explained where they are supposed to hide Siumek and Malka and where they would stay until they entered the hideout.

"You need to arrive late at night when everyone is fast asleep. Walk, but not on the main road. Someone might see you. Think of our offer. If you decide to accept, as soon as you arrive place a small stone on each step leading to the casino so we know in the morning you have arrived," Donia told Siumek and Malka.

After the girls left, Siumek spoke to his wife Malka in Yiddish, "*Die shikses wilen awek nemen fun uns wos inz omer noch, und ybergeben uns die Datchen.*" "These non-Jews want to take what is still in our possession and then hand us over to the Germans."

"Nonsense," Malka said. "This is G_d's finger. He has sent these girls to save us. I'm telling you there is a G_d. If they wanted to make money they would look for someone with money. Besides, one of them looks like a Jewish girl but she has blue eyes and the other one really looks like a non-Jew but she has Jewish eyes."

(At that time the Rainhartzes didn't know that the girls were not in touch with other Jews. That the girls were the only Jews of Bolechów they talked with.)

Since meeting with the Rainhartzes Donia was careful to get up early in the morning to go outside and see if there were stones on the casino steps.

One day the manager of the casino was restless and woke up early. She got out before Donia and saw the three stones. The manager wondered how these stones got there. Yesterday there were none.

She called in Ukrainian, "Donia, Donia. *A chto postavił try kamincy na schodach.*" (Who put the stones on the steps?)

Donia explained that there were children who played nearby. They must have left the stones. The manager shrugged her shoulders as one doubting, but accepted the answer regarding the mystery of the stones. The girls then knew that the Rainhartzes were in the agreed upon hiding place.

Several years later, after Malka's husband passed away, she described to me how all this happened.

"It was the middle of August 1943. We arrived quietly after the casino was closed. We put the stones on the steps as instructed and went to the basement of the abandoned synagogue next to the house where Siumek's parents once lived. As the girls told us, we had to stay in the basement until one of the girls showed up giving us a sign that we should move to the hay loft of the casino.

"Maryjka appeared in the morning with a big jug of milk and said, "Everything will be okay."

"The girls had put a ladder near the barn so we could climb up and settle in the pile of hay and sleep there.

We sat all day in the basement of the abandoned synagogue and planned our stay in our hideout. Siumek had seen where we would hide. He had prepared a large piece of cloth to put under our mattresses in order to insure that pieces of straw created by our weight would not fall between the cracks and land on the head of the people using the toilet which would betray our presence immediately. After we filled the bags with straw we brought them above the outhouse and settled there.

"On the second night, after midnight, when the town slept, we quietly sneaked from the basement of the synagogue and, using the ladder, we climbed up into the casino's loft.

"We couldn't escape the pungent smell of the animal's pen and the squeaking of pigs. We added this to our feeling of security. The noise of the pigs and their smell should keep people from coming closer.

"Fumbling, we found the bags, filled them with the straw that

152

was there. Afterward, we hid the bags under the hay. We climbed on the pile of hay and fell asleep out of exhaustion, probably partly from our tension.

"Early in the morning one of the girls came and woke us up. She said we should move the mattresses on top the outhouse. We had to move to the hiding place because Gawroński needed to bring hay down for the pigs.

"Carefully and quietly, with a knife, Siumek cut three planks that were not too thick. He cut them in a way that made them easy to put back into place discreetly. Siumek crawled through the opening inside the cloth he had bought and placed under the mattresses. After we were both inside Siumek carefully put the planks back as they were before. There was no sign of a hidden access.

"The size of the hideout was 2.50 meters long and 1.50 meters wide. Because of the slope of the roof, the height allowed us to only sit or lie down. We could not stand.

"We ate food with a hearty appetite in the dark, not knowing what we were eating. We whispered our impressions of the cook and of the food that was brought to us. Only in the morning if there were some leftovers we could see what we had been eating. Often nothing was left and we were always hungry. We brought hunger along from the camp so it was hard to satisfy it

"Thirst bothered us much more than hunger. We were often thirsty. It was difficult for the girls to bring water.

"The girls brought food and made it look as though they were feeding the pigs. Pigs do not consume water. They eat their food diluted. It happened more than once that someone showed up wanting to use the outhouse and Donia had to put our meal into the trough for the pigs. On such occasions our meal was delayed or did not come at all. But, usually, we got enough to eat.

"How could they bring water to the outhouse? Donia found a solution. Every day the girl going to the dairy to get milk would wash and rinse the bucket or the great pitcher and leave water in it. On the way out of the casino area the girl that was going to the outhouse and would transfer the water into a receptacle Siumek would hand her.

"This was one of the most dangerous activities of our rescue operation. The water transfer was carried out every day in full daylight during the morning. There was some concern. The casino manager could see everything from her window on the second floor. She could notice that the girl on the way to bring milk was entering the outhouse with a jug or a bucket in her hand. How come she didn't leave it outside?

"At night Malka told me they were to take turns sleeping, ready at any moment to shut the mouth of the other one with both hands if snoring started or if, G_d forbid, shouting in his sleep.

"Our toilet bucket was inside the hideout. "In order to throw out the contents of the bucket Siumek would raise three boards, lower the bucket and empty it directly into the outhouse. Of course this was done late at night. We did all that in complete silence. One of us watched through the cracks between the boards to make sure no one was approaching the toilets. We were never certain if someone would show up from the street or from the casino needing to use the outhouse. The whole time we were afraid that someone would hear our activity or noise and that this would trigger their curiosity. We didn't want to move during day. What if someone showed up to use the outhouse and the door was locked from inside and nobody came out? This would definitely raise great and justified suspicion

"On the other hand, late at night, when there was no movement of wagons around the casino and human voices were not heard, every individual noise, even the smallest, could be heard quite far away.

"The adjacent pigsty was somewhat reassuring for us. The noise from around the outhouse could be explained as being caused by the pigs. Human voices could lead us to an extermination camp.

"On Saturday nights when the Germans and the Ukrainian police would come to the casino, we had to be especially carefully. The worst drunkards were full of beer amd urinating around the barn and in the outhouse. But we could not rely on the fact that they were drunk. In spite of being drunk, they might hear something and let their imaginations roam free. It was necessary to keep very quiet. When someone entered the outhouse we just about stopped breathing. It was a terrible feeling.

"Tracking hidden Jews was in full swing. It was almost a game. The young Ukrainians and Polish *Folks Deutsche* made Jew tracking a hobby.

"The place was dark. We could see what was happening through the cracks between the boards. From outside it was impossible to see what was going on in the attic of the toilets. When we wanted to look outside we made sure not to bring our eye too close to the gap in the boards. We worried that the white of our eye might have been spotted by someone who would suspect that people were under the roof."

About a week after the Rainhartzes were settled in their hiding place, Malka and Siumek heard 900 shots that ended the lives of the last Jews in Bolechów.

(A remark from the author: Those were the Jews from several labor camps concentrated in a specially built "trap" by the German Grzymek, the liquidator of the Lwów ghetto, after he had promised the Jews hope and a future as described in the book *A Jew Again*.)

Malka knew that one of these shots ended her sister's life. She had entered the new camp having no alternative. (The author and his cousin Juzik, the only ones in their family to survive, were hidden in the nearby village of Gerynia, and also heard the shots.)

Donia learned that in this *aktion* the last Jews of Bolechów were killed. Only a few dozen were transferred to Stryj. (This is questionable because at that time the ghetto and labor camp were no longer in existence) Bolechów became *Judenrein*, free of Jews.

Donia and Malka Rainhartz (Miriam is the name she adopted in Israel) mentioned that, after the *aktion*, about 30 Germans arrived at the casino. Lunch had been prepared for them. A few of them went to the pump outside to wash their hands. Donia and Malka saw that the water that fell from their hands was red with blood.

Malka said, "I had to discard the water that was in the bowl. This haunted me for more than 20 years."

"Through the slots we looked at these murderers as they wash their hands stained by the blood of our family members and relatives. We clearly saw the color of the water that fell from their vile hands."

The casino manager had a sister who lived in a small town near Lwów. Once she came to visit her in Bolechów. This woman was married to a deacon. They had no children. The woman stayed for several days. When she saw how well Donia was working, she asked her to leave the casino and come with her.

"Come to us. We have a large fruit garden with lots of fruit and also a beautiful vegetable garden. You will have plenty," she said. "I understand you are an orphan. What does it matter to you where you are? Why don't you come with me?"

Donia thought to herself that if it were not for the Rainhartzes she might be tempted with this woman's proposition because it was a much safer place. Due to the current situation however, which she could not divulge, she couldn't agree to leave. She had committed herself to the lives of these two people. She once again used the excuse that being in her present position helped keep her away from the young people who sometimes bothered her.

"Ma'am, I whole heartedly would go with you but my friend Vaśko, who is working in Germany, knows this place and will come looking for me here. As soon as he gets some vacation, we will get married and go together to Germany."

This argument was most persuasive. Why should she get Donia for a short time when she was ready to go to Germany after the wedding and that could be very soon?

"I hope you will invite me to the wedding. I will bring you a beautiful gift," said the sister of the casino manager

Donia told me that she hadn't told this to anyone to his day and surely not to the Rainhartzes. The life of these two people was more important than her own life.

The manager of the casino had a daughter from a previous marriage. She lived in Stryj. She had a very Semitic face. Once, when she was on the train, she was arrested under the suspicion that she was Jewish. With great difficulty she was able to prove who she really was. Since then the manager's new husband took care of the problem. A police officer used to accompany her.

Miriam told me, "The husband of the casino manager Harasimov was a high ranking officer at the *Halyczyna* SS Division and used to come to the casino for breaks. He liked playing around with the pigs. He loved them. One afternoon as he was playing with the pigs in the yard a shot was heard. It brought us to the slits in the boards to see what was happening. We didn't find the cause of the shot but we saw Donia standing in front of the porch pale as a sheet. She was clutching a small carpet that she'd hung on the rail. The poor thing was trembling. She probably thought he had found us and shot us."

I asked Miriam, "How did you wash the latrine bucket? I understood from your story you didn't have enough water to drink?"

"To wash the bucket? To wash our bucket?" she asked twice. We didn't wash it at all. Where could we have found water? Sometimes we had nothing to drink. The stench from the outhouse also concealed the stench coming from the bucket. We made sure to cover it as much as possible.

The girls usually brought dry food. The casino manager rested in the afternoon. They would come to the outhouse with buckets in their hands full of food for the pigs. In the pockets of their apron was the food for the hideout. Donia made certain that the Rainhartzes would have enough for a whole day without her having to come back again with more food. You never knew in advance what could happen. A lot of Ukrainian policemen could arrive. Piatke with his vicious dog or too many Germans in transit might stop there.

Every time the manager went to Stryj Donia brought more supplies to the Rainhartzes trying to make sure their reserve would not diminish. The girls entered the outhouse and, after closing the door, would push up a board or two and hand the food through the opening.

The Rainhartzes had a difficult time with personal hygiene. They could not wash thoroughly; not even one time throughout the entire time they were hiding. The filth, the stench, and threat that they could be discovered at any moment were still preferred over death.

According to Miriam they never had lice and felt fortunate at least for this one small blessing. They had not brought them from the camp.

Siumek made sure to shave at least twice a week and this wasted nearly a full glass of water. Another extra glass of water was used every day for tooth brushing.

After two or three months in hiding, the casino manager received a letter from the Gestapo in Stanisławów. In the envelope the manager found instructions detailing an impending search of all structures and institutions belonging to the Germans. The directive was necessary, it was explained, because in Stanisławów, in a building next to the police station, a bunker hiding sixteen Jews was discovered. Consequently everyone had to do a search of their premises and surroundings to check if Jews were hiding.

At that time all the towns in the juridiction of Stanisławów and Lwów were already *Judenrein*, free of Jews. Urchins, who found themselves in the occupation of searching and identifying Jews on the road and in railway stations, now worked hard to find hidden Jews because they would get a prize from the Germans for their discovery.

Several months had gone by since the last Jews were murdered. And they, the hunters, found quite a few bunkers. Could it be that there were more Jews still hiding?

They wanted to find all the hidden Jews and hand them over to the Germans. G_d forbid a Jew remained alive.

A broad shouldered Ukrainian with a slight limp named Gawroński often visited the casino.

He occasionally entered the courtyard of the casino with his wagon which was pulled by two horses. He would unload a number of beer barrels brought from the Kalusz brewery from his wagon. On the steps to the basement Gawroński used to place a board. He would walk slowly in front of the barrel holding it with his back and hands to prevent it from rolling. The barrel slid and rolled according to Gawroński's direction. When the barrels were all in the basement he placed them exactly below the bar.

A long pipe descended from the ceiling. Gawroński opened the cap of one of the barrels and plunged a long pump with a handle into it. This connected the hose from the ceiling down to the pump and then he turned on the handle. He would start to pump air into the barrel. The pressure generated in the barrel brought the beer up to the bar. Garwroński rolled the empty barrels up the ramp, placed them on the cart and took them back to the brewery to be refilled.

Twice a week on Saturday and Sunday, a party took place at the Casino Ballroom. On those evenings the casino required Gawroński's services all the time. He had to come down to the cellar to inflate air into the barrel and replace an empty barrel with a full one. Gawroński had worked at the casino since its inception. It was a steady and secure income. He also did other delivery jobs for the casino and was well paid. His work at the casino was a side job. His main job was to carry logs from the forest and occasionally transport things for town residents.

Before the war Gawroński worked as a coachman for the Laznik brothers. They were Jews and owned a transport company. The Lazniks used several teams of horses and several carters worked for them. Laznik brothers built stables at the carter's and the horses were kept on the carter's property. Gawroński regularly managed freight from the railway station to all those factories that did not have a private railroad spur and received raw materials from abroad or from far away towns. Gawroński used to transport boards from the sawmill to the trader's yards.

In 1939, when the area was under Soviet occupation, in order not to be considered Capitalists, the Laznik brothers agreed with Gawroński that the pair of horses he led all the time should supposedly belong to him. Gawroński would pay the brothers 50% of his earnings when he used the horses and wagon.

By mid-1941 the area was occupied by the Germans, The Laznik Brothers horses remained in Gawroński's hands permanently. He didn't go to the brothers and offer to continue paying them as before or to buy the horses from them, nor the wagon and the stable that he was using because of the circumstances. His Ukrainians neighbors who always saw Gawroński with the same horses and using the same stable were ready to swear the horses had belonged to Gawroński for ages.

In the last year Gawroński suffered from terrible back pains and he limped slightly. There were no longer any Jewish doctors in Bolechów and Gawroński didn't know any other doctors.

Old women used to explain to him that he was suffering from rheumatic pains and that he got them when he carried the blocks of ice from the river to use in households. Others said he got it when he transported salted cattle skins from the train station to the many tanneries in town.

Gawroński's wife used grandmothers' remedies such as cabbage leaves and nettles to ease his pain. But, except for the painful stinging, they didn't help. He felt relief for only a short time. Could it be that the stinging pain from the nettles was strong and so his back felt some relief from his own aches?

Donia was present when the casino director turned to Gawroński and said, "Mr Gawroński, could it be that a Jew is hiding in one of our buildings?"

He asked, "Where did the idea suddenly come to your head? It isn't possible. The camp was surrounded at night and none of them managed to escape."

"Well, Mr Gawroński," the casino operator said, "I was instructed by the S.S. in Stanisławów to do a search. I would like you to do that search for me."

Donia stopped breathing. She needed to do something. But what? Again her diligence and quick thinking saved them. The idea of keeping pigs in the casino area proved to be a success. Having pigs allowed her to bring in food for the couple much more easily. The noise and bad odor they gave out provided cover in case the people in hiding made a careless move. In addition, it kept Piatke's fearsome dog at bay - not to mention that the Rainhartzes had better food rations thanks to the pigs.

Dilemmas of a Potential Partner to Murder

Donia was terrified. She didn't know what to do when she heard the order given to Gawroński by her boss. Donia suddenly thought of the piglets she had brought in only two weeks before. She first went to the barn and moved the ladder so Gawroński wouldn't think of going up to the hay piled up there and get too close to the thin wall that separated the couple from the rest of the barn. On that day Gawroński suffered a bad pain attack in his back. It was much worse than usual. Maybe it was the result of carrying heavy barrels to the basement only an hour ago. Or maybe it was because of the weather since there were clouds, a harbinger of rain. But he couldn't refuse the casino manager's request and oppose the Gestapo from Stanisławów.

He thought, "Maybe it is my lucky day and I will find someone hiding around here." He would be paid for this extra job. And if Jews were found he would also get a premium from the Germans

Gawroński decided to start the search in the attic of the casino. Limping slowly he climbed up the three floors. He climbed the last level with silent curses, grumbling in pain and anger after every step.

It was dark in the attic. He had never been there before. The idea of going back down and bringing up a flashlight didn't even pass through his head as he was still feeling the pain from the climb. He wanted to find a place to sit down immediately to ease the pain in his back. He walked two steps and came upon a beam. He sat right down. Sitting on the beam he thought that if he had to go down to get a flashlight he would not be able to make it up the stairs again.

He thought to himself that if he couldn't climb the stairs again the casino manager would ask someone else. What if Jews are really hiding here? The other one will get the money and not me. In fact I am not looking for a job to deliberately look for Jews. But why miss an opportunity?

Gawroński waited until his eyes grew accustomed to the darkness. Slowly he could distinguish different objects around him that were piled up without any order. There were old things from the past and probably dating back from the Jewish doctor Dr. Goldszlag's grandmother since they had owned the building a long time ago.

When he became used to the darkness Gawroński began to move carefully. Dust was everywhere. Every object he lifted created a cloud of dust making him cough and sneeze.

Every few meters he was obliged to cross over a beam that supported the roof. Raising his foot was very painful.

"Where on earth could Jews hide in here? After all this dust they could die within a month," he thought while moving another bookcase or an old heater. I haven't even seen a mouse so far. If Jews were hiding here somewhere they would have food and I would see mice or their droppings. I haven't seen one. Definitely, there are no Jews here."

"No Jews here. That's my conclusion" said Gawroński as he came close to the brick chimney. "Only two weeks ago Szlapak, the chimney sweeper, was here and he is an expert in finding Jews. He found at least three bunkers in the past months. No doubt he searched every inch up here in this attic."

Disappointed, Gawroński climbed slowly down the stairs. "Why aren't stairs always going down? It's a lot easier and there's almost no pain" he thought.

He went into the basement he knew so well. "And what shall I look for here? I am here at least twice a week, he thought. "But the command must be fulfilled. Maybe I didn't notice that Jews were hiding in the cellar beyond the beer barrels or some other junk."

Suddenly his eyes lit up. "What really happened to Dr. Goldszlag? Who saw him leave his house and move to the Jewish quarter? When was he killed? Could it be he found himself a hiding place in his house where he remains with his family, waiting for the war to come to an end? There I ran into a mouse every once in a while. There must be some food, a sign of a hideout. In this huge basement maybe there are areas I didn't search. Perhaps here is the place I will be lucky and get the German bonus for having discovered hidden Jews. Recently the Germans raised the bonus significantly for finding Jews, a rare phenomenon as the area was declared free of Jews. If I find Jews here the Jews will certainly give me a substantial sum in order not to betray them. Whatever the secret ransom, I will have to think what to do with it. It might be worth waiting for the extradition. The reward will be more important when there are no Jews at all."

Those were the dilemmas Gawroński's was mulling over.

He didn't know that the Soviets already took Dr. Goldszlag away from his home and gave him to one of the Commissars elected as the commander of the town

Gawroński walked up to a wall where an oil lamp hung from a nail. He shook it to check the level of the oil.

"A flashlight would do a better job," he thought. But the memory of the pain he had going up to the attic and the thought of going up the stairs again killed the idea of a flashlight.

Holding the oil lamp in one hand and a staff in the other, Gawroński began passing along the walls of the basement knocking every suspected beam in order to check if the wall was a fake. He worked slowly and carefully. It was not every day such an opportunity came up. He would be paid for the hours spent in the search. It would not be wasted time if he could find a hideout.

It was already noon when he finished the disappointing basement search. Limping even more, he went up the stairs into the hall. In addition to his disappointment, he was tired from walking along the big basement's walls and knocking on them.

In the lobby he met the director of the casino. Donia was nearby busy cleaning the tables.

The casino manager turned to Gawroński and asked, "What was that stomping I heard coming from the basement?"

"I was looking for a hiding place behind a fake wall. In my opinion it is the only place of all the places in the yard that could provide a hideout for Jews. But now I'll have a little rest and then check the hayloft though I don't think there could be a hideout up there."

A Pig that Saved Jews

"Donia, please give Mr Gawroński a cup of tea and something to eat."

Donia gave Gawroński a plate of potatoes with some goulash, poured him a cup of tea and, as the manager left, she also gave him a double vodka.

"Maybe he will fall asleep and forget about searching the hayloft. Maybe I have hypnotic powers and I can make him sleep," she thought, watching him gulp down his food. He looked satisfied and praised the goulash and the fried potatoes.

Donia could not numb Gawroński's senses. The vodka he drank was a wasted effort.

He got up from the table, happy and well fed. The pain somewhat weakened, he wiped his moustache and turned to go to the barn. Donia followed him. But when he entered the barn, Donia went to the pig pen, caught one piglet and began to choke it.

The pig started shrieking and screaming terribly and Donia started screaming too.

"Mr Gawroński, Mr Gawroński, please save my little pig. I have to fatten it and return it to the authorities. What will happen if it chokes?"

Gawroński came down the ladder, took the pig from Donia's hands and said, "Apparently he has something in his throat."

Gawroński lifted the piglet firmly. Miraculously the piglet stopped screaming. Together with the relaxation of the pig, G_d made Gawroński forget to complete his search in and around the hay loft. He reported to the manager that he had thoroughly searched and that she could take it easy. "There is no hiding place in your area that hides even one Jew."

Donia blessed G_d for his help though the help came through a *non-kosher* animal.

During all this time Maryjka was busy cleaning rooms and other cleaning chores rather than being anywhere near Gawroński, the manager or Donia. She heard the manager read the instructions received from the Gestapo in Stanisławów and decided to distance herself from the whole thing.

Following the search instructions and the tension it brought, Maryjka got cold feet. She began to fear the discovery of the hidden Jews and all of them being murdered together.

That evening she whispered to Donia, "This tension is unbearable. The Gestapo directive goes to all institutions including Town Hall where the police headquarters are located. Recently too many German and Ukrainian police are here. Piatke, the policeman, and his dog that was trained to spot Jews, are showing up here more and more often. Now, by order of the Gestapo, they will look even harder everywhere in town. Eventually they will find them and it will be our end too because we hid them and gave them food."

"And what is your intention?" asked Donia quietly and fearfully.

"I have already found another workplace at the orphanage outside the fence. This is a place that has nothing to do with the Jews in the casino area."

Donia said, "I resigned myself. I decided to save the Rainhartzes, whatever happens. I am asking you not to talk to anyone about the hiding of the Jews, even if you work somewhere else and the Rainhartzes are discovered here. They may tell after being tortured that you have provided them with food."

"Yes, I am well aware of this danger. I will help you as much as I can. But there is too much tension here. I cannot be here all the time."

The following day Maryjka came up to the boss and said, "I didn't want to tell you because I was afraid you wouldn't let me continue working here."

"What are you hiding from me?" the casino manager raised her voice.

"I am ill and the doctor forbids me to work hard. The work is very hard for me here. Please forgive me and please allow me to start working at the nearby orphanage where the work will be easier for me."

"If you are ill and it is difficult to work here then you may go. Keep working until the end of the month. I shall give you your wages and then go to them."

Maryjka went to work at an orphanage near the casino. After a few days she told Donia, "If the Jews are found, I will have nothing to do with it. I am not working at the casino and nobody can link me to these Jews. Even if they tell I provided them with food, they don't know who I am and where I disappeared to. It would be your problem. You will take the whole responsibility."

The orphanage in Bolechów

Despite what Maryjka said she did not completely ignore her responsibility. She worked at the orphanage. Winter was beginning. The couple's hiding place was not insulated at all. The walls were made of thin boards not tightly set and the cold came in. The cracks between the boards allowed in the cold wind and rain at all times.

The cold began to exasperate the Rainhartzes. They didn't move at all as it could have made noise and this had to be prevented at all costs. But too much lying around with no exercise or even movement deteriorates bones and muscles. When the wind blew hard and brought along rain there was no place to hide. They moved away from the cracks as much as they could and yet they were freezing. They felt the cold especially when they had to use the bucket when they needed to relieve themselves.

They thought of filling up the cracks with something but they were afraid that somebody outside may notice the change. When the bright days of frost replaced the autumn rain they found layers of ice in the cracks of their hiding place.

The cold made the cracks between the boards expand as if to help the wind and allow it to invade the hideout even more.

Everything seemed to be against the Jews at that time. Even the weather was against them.

One day when the casino director was not home Maryjka came to visit Donia. "What's up?" she asked.

Donia told her the couple was suffering from the cold. All the blankets they had brought along were not enough to keep them warm. Maryjka promised to explore the possibility of getting them a duvet or two.

One night after midnight, somebody suddenly entered the outhouse. It was unusual. Siumek put his hand over Malka's mouth. She understood immediately that some danger was up. Suddenly they heard a whisper, "Sha, sha. It is me, Maryjka." She began to lift the boards where the food was brought in.

While Siumek helped her move the boards to the side, Maryjka gave him two quilts she'd taken from the orphanage. She put her head into the hiding place and asked: "How do you feel? Do you need me to bring anything else?"

"First thank you for saving us from the cold. If you could get us a book or two, we could read. That would be great. It would help pass the time and give us something to do."

"I'll see what I can do," Maryjka said before she left the Rainhartzes.

Siumek and Malka now covered themselves with the quilts and felt the blood in their veins start flowing again.

Dawn arrived and they could see the quality of the quilts. Malka said, "He who steals from a thief is forgiven."

"What do you mean?" asked Siumek softly.

"These blankets were certainly stolen from the Jews and now they are saving us from the cold."

Maryjka stayed honest and asked Donia if she was providing the couple with food and all that they needed. Once she even jokingly said, but with a serious face, she would complain to the Gestapo that Donia was not bringing them enough.

This statement of exoneration, even as a joke, worried Donia. During the months they spent together Donia noticed that Maryjka was a strange woman. Because of her mood swings Donia worried that she would do something foolish.

A few days after she'd brought them the quilts she visited the couple again late at night. She poked her head up into their hiding place and asked, "How do you manage"

"We have no words to thank you sufficiently for bringing those quilts," they whispered back. "The temperature must have been about ten degrees below zero. Without the blankets you would have found two corpses. What was the reaction at the orphanage when they discovered some duvets were missing?"

"Believe me," she said, "If I took another two they wouldn't even know," Maryjka replied.

"What do you mean? Children without blankets because of us?"

"Don't be naïve. I didn't take away anything from the children. There is a blanket warehouse waiting for orphans to arrive. Because of the war they should not wait too long to have orphans showing up. You think in terms relating to Jews. For us Ukrainians the war didn't change anything. We continue a normal everyday life. You requested a book as you are bored. I brought Malka wool and knitting needles for you to knit a pair of socks and gloves for the casino manager. And for Siumek I have a book. I hope he will like it.

"And you will tell the casino manager it is a gift from the Jewish people who are bored in the attic of the outhouse of the casino she runs?"

"What's with you? We will tell her that either Donia or I knitted them at night. Now good night. I will come in a few days when I can put my hands on another book for you. In the end you will come out of here more educated than when you entered."

"Right. The everlasting stench of the toilet and the pig pen will improve our wisdom," the Rainhartzes joked back

A few days later Malka gave Donia a pair of gloves she had

been knitting. Donia knew from Maryjka that Malka had been knitting. She asked Maryjka to provide some skeins of wool to put in her room in case the casino manager entered her room. Donia took the gloves and told the manager she had been knitting them.

The manager was pleasantly surprised and asked, "What else can you do? Your Vaśko will be the happiest man."

The manager said, "You work alone, without Maryjka, and still managed to knit? At the end of the day you must be falling off your feet."

Donia realized she'd make a mistake. When on earth did she find time to knit? She replied, "I know the winter here and always knew gloves would be useful. I began knitting more than two months ago, a bit every night until I finished them."

"I noticed you go to the pump to get water without covering your hands. These gloves will keep you warm. If you knit another pair before the end of the winter, they will be for me."

"I will ask Maryjka, who has less work, to start knitting a pair for you now."

Knitting for Malka was like therapy, easing her strained nerves. Knitting kept her busy and kept away sad thoughts.

When Maryjka visited the Rainhartzes she understood Malka's situation. She brought another skein of wool and asked Malka to knit warm socks for her and Siumek to keep them warm.

"How come I didn't think of this before?" thought Maryjka.

"And where did you get the wool?" asked Malka.

"I unraveled old sweaters that would have gone into the garbage. A number of the cotton balls that were given to the orphanage to teach the girls how to knit found their way here," Maryjka replied.

"Since you brought us the quilts and it is not too cold, the first socks I knit I'd like to give to you and Donia. Will you wear them?"

"I'll bring you more wool so you will be busy."

Donia was very scared of Piatke's trained dog. She had heard about the ferociousness of that dog who was able to find

Jews in incredible hiding places. She was concerned about the Rainhartzes presence in the outhouse and the pigsty that was stuck to one of its walls. She wanted to make certain to confuse the dog's sense of smell. Donia secretly bought black pepper powder and scattered it around the outhouse every time she went there.

Even today Donia doesn't know for sure what confused the dog's sense of smell; if it was the stench of the outhouse, the pigsty, or the black pepper sprinkled around. Donia made sure to always carry a small amount of black pepper in her pocket which would also hinder his skill in finding out about her. Donia is inclined to believe that the pepper confused the dog.

To back up her theory she told me that for the 1943 Christmas Party Piatke came with his terrifying dog. They were all eating, drinking and celebrating full blast. Suddenly the dog, which was sitting near the heater, became agitated. Donia was helping with the service at this party. She thought that, despite the pepper in her pocket, the dog discovered she was Jewish. She was as pale as chalk. She thought that in a few more seconds he would sink his sharp teeth into her flesh. This would have been the end of her and also the Rainhartzes. She wasn't worried about herself as she didn't mind dying. But she was concerned for those under her protection. She was supposed to save them. She was really scared for them.

"Had the Germans killed me nobody in the world would have known my story, would have been sorry for me, or remembered me as no one in my family was alive," she thought. "What will happen to the Rainhartzes? Who will bring them food? How long would they last? Even if they snatch food from the pig trough during the night, where will they get water?"

Donia worried. Gawroński's search alarmed Maryjka. When she learns what happened to me she will probably stop coming to help the Rainhartzes.

Piatke noticed his dog's nervousness. He looked at him for a second and then they both left.

"I stood petrified. I didn't dare go to a mirror to check how pale I was. I had to start moving or be suspected. I came to the

170

realization that the dog didn't find out I was Jewish. The dog, despite the stench and the pepper, certainly ran to the outhouse. Piatke will come in a moment leading Siumek and Malka. He will take the three of us and, as in the past winter, he will lead us to death. *Hashem*, please be with us tonight.

No, tonight Piatke is at a party. He will not give up on the party. He will earn additional honor with the great success of his hero dog. He will deliver us to a junior officer, ordering him to watch us. And tomorrow he will lead us to the cemetery to kill us.

The tension lasted a long time. Donia tried to go about her tasks but the tension sabotaged her effort. She expected the worst but in the meantime tried to figure out what was going on.

Piatke was certainly investigating them to know who initiated the stay in this place and how was the food provided for them. Would he discover Maryjka's participation? If the Rainhartzes don't give Maryjka away, what will they say? They cannot point to the casino manager as the one who hid them and gave them food. They know her husband is a senior officer in the *Waffen SS Halyczyna*. Would Piatke believe them if they said she ordered them to hide in the outhouse of her casino?

Maybe they will tell him they alone took the initiative to hide there in the lion's den. Siumek knew of it from the time he used to handle the accounting books and found this safe place to hide. Every time he came to collect the management books he would first enter the outhouse and store everything from clothing or blankets in the attic that they would need when it was time to go into hiding. Siumek used to go out at night in search of food and would steal from the animals and the pigs. Not a bad cover story. They should have thought about it before.

But as old people say, "The farmer is smart after the damage is done."

Donia continued worrying. Would Piatke believe them? Certainly not. Now the battle is over. Will he be happy to kill the three of us or will he also kill the casino manager? Donia wasn't worried about her. Her husband, an officer in the *Waffen SS Halyczyna* will know how to save her.

Piatke may also recognize the quilts stolen from the orphanage and so he will find Maryjka. This assumption was almost impossible as no signs were on the quilts as they were manufactured by small manufacturers in Bolechów or in a neighboring town but Donia worried about it nonetheless.

Should she run and warn Maryjka? Her legs weighted a ton and she couldn't move, not even one step. Suddenly the door opened. There, in the doorway, stood Piatke with his dog. Piatke sat down on a chair near the stove and started petting the dog while talking to him. "You are a good dog. To the party's guests he said, "See how clever he is. He sensed there was something alive out there."

At that moment Donia sat down exhausted. She thanked G_d who, she believed, despite all her crimes, did not forget her and performed a *Chanukah* miracle.

A Ukrainian named Berezdivin was a handy man on call for the casino. He came when it was necessary to fix anything mechanical. Once, completely intoxicated, he came to repair the pump in the yard as it had suddenly stopped pumping water. Donia went out with him to show him that in spite of activating the lever, no water came out.

The man stood at the pump and staggered, lurched and flapped his arms around. Donia spoke to him while operating the lever. "Mr Berezdivin, can you see, no water is running here?"

Berezdivin looked at the pump and said, "You don't have to show me. I know the pump is broken. That's why I was asked to come here."

Suddenly, without any connection to the pump or water story, he turned to Donia and said, "Donia, I know everything about you."

Donia's world fell to pieces. What does he know and where did she go wrong? Could it be he was sitting next to the outhouse when she passed something to the Rainhartzes or simply exchanged a word with them?

Berezdivin continued, "The conscientiousness you show with your work, the hours you devote to this place show that you are not a Ukrainian. You pretend to be one but actually you must

172

be Jewish. They way you work is not at all like a typical Ukranian. I've noticed that about you."

Donia grew pale. Although the man was intoxicated, he told her that in the past he'd worked in France. Perhaps he learned there how to figure out who was a Jew?

Donia didn't answer him. She didn't lose her composure. It had been too many months of endeavors and efforts performed alone on the theatre of life's stage to be put off balance.

Donia pretended not to hear Berezdivin. She went to the casino and poured a big glass of vodka and brought it to Berezdivin, the chronically thirsty drunk.

Donia came up to him and said, "Excuse me but I have never seen you fix a pump before. As they say in our village, the damage is trembling with fear in front of a professional. For your professionalism I brought you a glass of vodka."

She thought, "If after drinking this glass he keeps talking, his words will be considered that of a drunk who is not quite himself and doesn't know what he is talking about."

Donia didn't know how to abruptly change her working behavior. She thought she was working like a typical Ukrainian who say they are diligent and the Jews idlers. She thought, "If I am not lazy it takes away the basic suspicion. And here comes this drunk and he destroys the Ukrainian Nationalist anti-Semitic theory."

Since the municipality had declared Bolechów free of Jews, fantasies about finding hidden Jews overcame individuals. Everyone wanted to be a hero. Fantasy had no limits. Even Berezdivin imbibed the fantasy in one of the pubs and now was trying it on Donia. "Or maybe he is absolutely right and my submissive behavior is detrimental," she thought.

Berezdivin drank the vodka and forgot what he was saying. While swaying in all directions he managed to fix the pump, was paid, and went home

Several weeks passed during which time Berezdivin showed up at least once or twice a week. He never spoke again about his suspicion which could have been fatal to her and the couple. Donia started to relax a little.

Donia was different from Maryjka. Donia was hard working and did not curse like simple Ukrainian women do. Donia's refinement could really be a major problem.

There were many rumors in the spring of 1944. Everyone was talking about the Germans and that they would probably not prevail. Germans drivers were stopping at the casino nearly on a daily basis. They were transporting equipment, which German engineers dismantled, before ceding the land back to the Soviets.

On the radio they were announcing that the winning German army had improved their positions.

Even the mood of the Rainhartzes got better and better. Liberation day was not far. The front was getting closer.

There was a rumor in town that a group of 16 Jews hiding in caves in the forest of Bubniszcze encountered a partisan unit led by General Kołpak. The partisans were on their way to blow up oil facilities in Borysław and Drohobycz. The Jews in hiding came out of their caves and joined the partisans who were surprised to find Jews in the woods and not in a ghetto or a camp.

This rumor, even if it was not certain, alarmed the local Ukrainians who had been active in the killings of Jews. They recently heard what happened in the town of Skalat where partisans took over the town and shot 60 collaborators and 40 Germans who opposed the partisans.

How many people served under this General Kołpak? Just a month ago he was in the Ternopol area. Now he is here in the Bubniszcze woods. Who actually will defend the town of Bolechów if a partisan unit decides to conquer the town? Will the two and a half policemen be able to stand up against a unit of partisans? Perhaps Bandera's group will come and protect the town. Bandera's group are not fit for an open fight with an organized force. Where was Bandera when Babij's gang entered town in an attempt to eliminate the policeman Matwyjecki?

It would be interesting to learn which town those 16 Jews who joined the partisans came from. G_d forbid they came from Bolechów. What will really happen to us if this partisan unit captures the town? They certainly will slaughter all of us in revenge for what we did to their children and all their families here. Thus spoke the people of the town.

Every day in town we could hear the story of a Polish family who had moved west, well into Poland.

Among the first who moved west were those whose clean conscience warned them of reprisals by the approaching Red Army. They feared that if a Jew were left alive he would remember what they did to his family and to other Jews. Bandera's nationalistic Ukrainian gang started to murder Polish people in the villages. Following the Poles who moved were the western Ukrainians who feared the vengeance of the surviving Jews. Finally the Ukrainian police also began to flee westward.

The first to escape among the Ukrainian police was the killer Matwyjecki. He sent his wife and son first. Then he threw away his police uniform and replaced it with a business suit that he kept ready at all times. He carried a small suitcase full of jewelry, gold coins, dollars bills and sterling. All this he robbed from the Jews before he killed them and left Bolechów. Through Lwów, Kraków, Prague, Germany, Belgium and France he went. He fled to Canada with his family. (He escaped being arrested in Bochnia, near Kraków in 1946: See *A Jew Again*, by Shlomo Adler)

The next policeman who ran away was Lukovoj who arrived somehow in Great Britain. Nazi hunters and their collaborators tried to kill him in the early sixties.

The Front suddenly stopped advancing. The Germans carried out counter attacks, and the Red Army withdrew from several cities. Several hundred Jews who had come out of hiding were murdered by the mob. They'd been brainwashed by the authorities into believing that their cities were free of Jews. They'd been ready, with their luggage packed, thinking they could escape to the west. They began unpacking and returned to their hiding places.

There is nothing like the German Army. The Soviets didn't realize who they were dealing with.

Bandera members and the extreme Ukrainian nationalists, who had no more Jews to murder or to deliver to the Germans after wiping out their belongings, started murdering the Poles. They started to look for Polish properties which, because of the

German occupation, were worth more. Even some of the Poles had not behaved morally. They had robbed the Jews directly or took Jewish property for themselves that was left with them until the storm passed. For the remaining Jews in hiding, rage had already passed. No one would ask for the return of their property. Why wouldn't the soon to be established independent Ukraine be free of Poles as well? The Jewish property then would be in the correct hands; Ukrainian hands.

Not a day passed without news of a Polish family murdered in one of the nearby villages or suburbs. Polish villagers started to seek refuge in town centers. But this did not save them. They were robbed of their property and ran penniless to the west.

Proximity and Salvation

Three weeks before the liberation by the Red Army the casino manager called Donia and said, "My husband was not home for over a month. Yesterday he called and asked me to go to Kraków. I am leaving tomorrow. If you need anything you will need to contact Mr. Hucalo, the mayor. He will provide for your needs."

The next day, after the manager left, Donia became executive director of the casino. Donia was alone in the casino building. The director's apartment was locked. Therefore Donia stopped cleaning the three rooms in the upper floor. Suddenly she had free time.

Ukrainians and Poles did not come for a beer on Saturday and Sunday. And Gawroński didn't bring beer barrels from Kałusz anymore.

Donia started visiting the outhouse more often, spending more time there. She shut herself up inside and, standing on the seat, moved the two boards aside and put her head into the hideout. Every so often she brought the Rainhartzes an apple or a sandwich with meat. But mostly she told them about the mood in town and what the residents said about the approaching front.

"Where do you get this news?" they once asked Donia.

"At the dairy or the stores, where I take the eggs. I hear what people are talking about."

"Does Piatke keep coming to the casino?" asked Siumek.

"He must have been the first to run away," she responded with pleasure. "I also think the casino manager has gone and will not return. She feels that, thanks to her husband, the "Righteous" and the rest, she will be number one of the *persona non grata* on the Soviet's list."

"What bandits besides Piatke fled?" they asked.

"I heard that Matwyjecki and Łukovoi have also gone."

"In other words there is no rule in place?" concluded Siumek

"It is not just like that. Hucalo, the mayor, and the director are sitting there arranging everything as if nothing is going to happen," she told them. "The Agricultural Institute that gave us the pigs is operating normally. If the casino manager isn't back before the end of next week, then I will bring the pig that has reached the required weight to the Institute myself."

"Why are you going to give them back a pig? The Russians are about to arrive here. It isn't certain we will have food right away and the pig could fill in for this lack."

"And who will slaughter it for me? The Pole Szymanski? He was afraid of the Bandera gang and took off for Poland. Up until now I used to bring him the pig. He weighted it. He considered the costs and would give us sausages and meat. He was an honest person. I heard his brother's son was shot in Stryj prison under the eyes of his mother. He was taken to Stryj after Jews were discovered hiding in the basement of the teacher Szydłowska's house. He used to come there every evening with a basket of food. It was said that he would bring the food because, among the hiding Jews, was a beautiful girl he was in love with.

This was the substance of the conversations held between Donia and the Jewish couple hidden in the attic of the outhouse.

In the casino manager's room there was a telephone. But the room was locked. The director of the casino was in such a rush to meet her husband that she forgot to tell Donia who to call when help was needed.

Donia herself had no one to call. Her family no longer existed and Vaśco, the boyfriend she'd invented, was only in her imagination.

Phones were big and awkward and still a luxury in those days. Not everyone could afford to keep such a wonder at home. Even the infrastructure didn't exist. In order to contact somebody by phone (if you had one) you had to turn a small handle which allowed you to connect to the town operator. Then you had to ask the operator to connect you to the operator in the other town and then you would give her the number you wanted. This is how it worked. The operator was the one connecting you. Even if no one else was on this line at that particular moment, the operator could hear your conversation.

Donia wouldn't know where or who to call even if the phone had been at hand. Donia only remembered that she was to contact Mayor Hucalo if she needed anything.

German drivers carrying fuel and other supplies from Romania occasionally entered the casino. Donia brought them sandwiches and tea or coffee just as they used to get before. When Donia needed something she turned to the mayor's office and obtained all that she required directly from them.

On the second week of Donia's temporary casino management, she brought the plump pig to the Agricultural Institute where she had gotten it two months before.

"Oh, you brought a fattened pig. It is not bad," said the clerk after evaluating it and finding it weighted 40 kilos. "You know you are the only one to have brought back a pig. Other people feel the German occupation is drawing to an end and they prefer to keep the pig for themselves. People don't know what will happen when the Russians come again. With the Russians will return the Żydy (a disrespectful name for Jews) who fled with them and they will demand their property back. We will have a big mess here if we survive after the front comes through this zone. The Germans have built protective lines on the Świca, the Sokal and the Stryj Rivers. No doubt some fierce fighting will take place here. People say that before the Russians took control in Tarnapol county intense combat took place and caused many civilian casualties."

"What shall I do with the pig?" Donia tried to return to the subject. She wanted to go and share the good news with the

Rainhartzes. The Russians were close and would be there very soon.

"The manager left. There are no instructions about the casino. When she returns I might as well go to my village. The Germans will stop patronizing the casino," she said.

"Why should your manager return when all those with a distressed conscience fled westward? And your manager's husband was a "Righteous." The Russians would hang him first if they caught him here. You don't know what his role was in the *Halcyczyna* SS Divison, do you?"

"I don't know. I wasn't interested. I worked here like a dog from dawn to dusk. The director was a nice woman. But she could have at least let me know she wasn't coming back. Well whatever happens, let's hope we manage to survive in peace."

Donia wanted to leave. But the woman at the Agricultural Institute stopped her. It was boring for her to sit alone and now she had someone to talk to. She wanted to take advantage of it.

"This pig was lucky. It seems he had a good time at the casino. War was raging around and it put on weight. It lacked for nothing."

"And why should it have lacked food? The German soldiers also didn't know what hunger meant. They left half sandwiches which the pigs enjoyed. I must go back there now. Maybe a driver will show up and nobody is there to hand him a cup of tea or a stronger drink."

Encouraged by what she heard at the Agricultural Institute, Donia happily and cheerfully went back to the casino. If she wasn't ashamed she would have pranced and romped as she did when she was a child. She had to remind herself to be careful. She still had to act correctly and not draw attention to herself. She didn't want to ruin things at this last minute.

When she entered the courtyard of the casino she first went to the outhouse. She couldn't resist. She had to bring the good news to the Rainhartzes. That piece of news made Donia run several times to the outhouse to be sure the couple understood the meaning. The coming redemption was felt in town.

The girls at the dairy told her that citizens were not allowed to take trains in any direction. People who somehow came from Lwów told *Bihme* (Ukrainian for a swear like G-d is my witness) they heard artillery barrages with their own ears. Within the past five years they saw withdrawals of the hosts: the Polish Army, the Red Army, and now the retreating German Army. These people knew about a retreat and its meaning.

To the disappointment of some residents, the town had no warehouses full of supplies as in 1939 or in 1941. They were empty. The Germans didn't suffer from overabundance this last year. The farmers lagged in providing a percentage of their crops and various partisans had looted supply convoys and warehouses.

It was a *fait accompli*. It was a sure thing. The German army would leave the area soon. "Experts" even said the war would be over within a few months. The women talked wherever Donia went.

Maryjka rarely visited. She was afraid that she might make a mistake at the last moment and be captured along with the fugitives. Maryjka was nervous. Donia began to wonder about Mariyjka's true identity. Maybe she wasn't Jewish after all? How was it possible not to see on her face the feelings that Donia felt inside? How come the defeat of the Germans and upcoming liberation were not affecting her?

Donia kept working as usual. She tried to hide her joy as if salvation did not interest her. Her entire focus was on not being caught at the last minute. She acted like Maryjka. It was not the time to reveal her true identity.

The fighting front was approaching. Occasionally a Soviet aircraft flew over the town firing cannons and *Katyusha* rockets.

For two days nobody entered the casino and Donia tried not to leave the yard. There were no people around. Everyone who remained in Bolechów tried to be close to or in their homes.

Donia heard the thunder of the battle around Bolechów. She heard the noise of the *Katyusha* rockets and explosions. She suddenly began to worry. She'd managed to survive until now. She prayed that G_d would prevent shells from hitting the building where she slept or, heaven forbid, the barn and the outhouse where the Rainhartzes were still hiding.

The Liberation and Confession

Finally the Russian troops entered the town of Bolechów. The news was brought to her by Maryjka who had heard it from a woman working with her at the orphanage.

"*Ya widiła Ruskich*," ("I saw the Russians,") she told Maryjka. Donia herself later saw the Red Army Cavalry Patrol Unit.

The liberation day was the saddest for Donia and Maryjka. Instead of jumping and being happy the two girls hugged each other the whole day and cried when they revealed each other's true identity.

Then Maryjka, to Donia's utmost surprise, told her about the girl who came before her to look for work at the casino. She said, "Do you remember the girl who came and asked for a job at the casino a couple of weeks before I arrived?"

"Of course I remember," replied Donia. She added, "How lucky I am that you came instead. I could not have saved the Rainhartzes with the other one."

"Donia, on the contrary, she was a much better person than me."

"And how do you know? You haven't even seen her."

"I saw her often. She was my late sister," replied Maryjka.

"What do you mean late? Dear God! Why didn't she come back?" asked Donia.

"I'll tell you and you will understand," replied Maryjka.

"My sister also had Aryan papers. After she was accepted for work here she returned home, prepared her things, said she'd found a job at the German casino in Bolechów and that she was heading there. My sister told me she had been observing the casino for two days. It seemed to her a safe place. Mostly German and Ukrainian policemen were around. Therefore no one would suspect a Jewish girl would want to take the risk of staying in such a place: in the lion's den.

"My sister said the casino manager and her assistant were nice people. They didn't even ask her name. My sister even suggested I too should have gone there and try to get a job. But the tragedy occurred when she was on her way to Bolechów. Someone probably suspected her and handed her over to the Ukrainian police. The Ukrainian police gave her to the Germans and they murdered her. When I learned that, in spite of my immense sadness, I realized there was a job available, even if it was in the lion's den.

"I knew what happened to my sister so I accepted the job on the condition that if the girl returned I would leave the workplace in her favor since she'd been promised the job. I knew of course she would not make it back."

As the Red Army Cavalry entered the yard of the casino the Rainhartzes came out of their hiding place. Siumek came up to the first horseman, who happened to be the closest to him, and kissed his boots. The horseman was embarrassed. He didn't understand what this man wanted from him. "W*y spasły naszu żyzń.*" "You saved our lives," said Siumek to the startled horseman.

The Rainhartzes had been hiding above the outhouse for about 13 months. After they stretched and put their bones back in order they went to the town center. In the town square they met Beno Reisman who had also survived. He was left alone. He'd had lost his only son and his wife who were murdered in the first *aktion* in Bolechów.

Beno left his hideout two days before. He immediately went to where he lived in the past. To his surprise he found the flat unoccupied and in a condition revealing that the people who were living there left in a panic, leaving everything behind.

Beno asked one of the remaining Polish neighbors close by who had lived in the apartment. The man replied, "It was a person who had no acquaintances, no friends. A despicable character. Until the last moment he was convinced the Germans would not withdraw from the town. Later on he gave in and left with his wife and a young child."

Beno entered the apartment, cleaned it and opened the windows. Then the authorities officially gave him back his apartment. On that same day he went to the town's square,. There he met the Rainhartzes. Beno invited them to his apartment. A few days later Donia joined them as well.

Donia's partner in this heroic exploit, Maryjka, was really named Fridka. She's decided to completely forget about her Jewishness. Two days after their liberation by the Red Army and the mutual disclosure of their identities, their paths separated. Fridka went back to her village, Kolczyce, and Donia never heard from her again.

The casino manager's room remained locked with all that remained inside. It didn't cross Donia's mind to break into the room and see all the property that the manager's husband stole from Jewish people.

She referred to her as the lady. When she spoke of her Donia suggested that the lady appreciated her.

Two days after the liberation, Donia went to the municipality. She handed the casino keys to Mayor Hucalo. Donia's admiration was great when the mayor's heavily pregnant maid opened the door. The maid was carrying his baby. And was still loyal to him.

It was the same Hucalo, the notorious anti-Semite, who served as head of the town during the Nazi era and was still the mayor now. The story of the mayor's mistress, Donia had heard a few months before. The people patronizing the casino, including Gawroński, loved this story about the bastard to be born.

Now Donia had the pleasure of seeing in person the woman around whom the juicy stories circulated. These stories were probably true for the most part since she was the mistress who took the keys Donia handed over.

After giving back the keys Donia went to the apartment where the Rainharz couple settled and stayed with them for a few days. The three of them sat for hours, talking in Yiddish, telling about their murdered families.

Malka said to Donia, "The first time I saw you I suspected you were Jewish because *Aza Gite neshome kan nisht zein bar a nyszt a Yid.*" (Such a good soul cannot be in a non-Jewish body.)

"It was lucky you trusted me and not some Ukrainian or German police. Otherwise we wouldn't be here. I don't know how I would have reacted if somebody had come up to me and said, "You are Jewish." I wouldn't have known how to get out of a dangerous situation. I knew all the Christians prayers which I had memorized before I came to Bolechów in preparation for my stay here. But who knows how I would have acted or reacted if I was really challenged. If I was in trouble would I be able to use my *chutzpah* (nerve) and utter some words of reproach; how did he dare suspect me?

"Indeed I found that kind of *chutzpah* in front Brezdivin, the drunk, when he told me he knew everything about me when he was at the water pump. I brought him a big glass of vodka and he forgot all about it. It haunted me for several weeks. It also happened when I explained to the priest who came to visit the casino manager. He asked how a Ukrainian country girl spoke so well."

Tears of joy and sorrow flowed from their eyes. They all could not believe their luck. They had survived. It had not been easy. But they were strong. And now they were alive.

Donia and Malka after the liberation

The Search for Survivors

After two days Donia boarded a train to Stryj. Deep down she hoped her uncle, the one who arranged for her to have Aryan papers, escaped and survived too. After all, he was a smart man. He had foreseen what was coming. Since he knew how to use his connections to get her Aryan papers he must have thought of a solution for his family.

Donia wanted to go back to her village, Synowódzko Niżne, to see if some of her Jewish neighbors had survived. Perhaps a friend from school and maybe someone from her family was still living. Maybe she could find out about the people who were on the train with her.

When the train reached Stryj, Donia met Mr. Pulsa, the Polish conductor. She knew him from before the war when she commuted daily to school.

Pulsa recognized her and exclaimed, "Jesus!" You are alive. Who apart from you survived?"

Donia told Pulsa that she had just arrived in Stryj. Her parents and all her immediate family perished in the Bełżec extermination camp. She explained that she wanted to go to town to check if her mother's brother Joseph Heller, his wife Malcia and their two children Meilech and Pepcia managed to survive. She also wanted to go to the village to see if any of her friends or maybe some family members survived.

Pulsa told her what the Ukrainians did in the village to their Jewish neighbors, even before they were assembled in the Stryj ghetto.

Hearing what Pulsa said she decided not to go to her village.

In Stryj she met several Jewish survivors and among them a relative, Yonah Friedler and his wife Sonia. She did not find Uncle Joseph and his family who she had hoped to find alive.

Disappointed not to find anyone in her extended family she went to Sambor. This town was where her father's brother Haim Pikholtz was living but none of them had survived.

In order to be close to where most of her family lived so as not to miss a family member who could have survived, she decided to stay in Sambor. She remained there for about 10 months until the summer of 1945. To make a living she worked in a restaurant where meals were served to the Communist Party Members.

When Donia understood that a miracle did not take place, and nobody from her family survived, she decided to use the right for repatriation that was reserved for Polish citizens according to the agreements signed in 1943 between the Russian and the Polish temporary government. She went to Kraków in Poland with a few Jewish survivors she'd met in Sambor. They were on their way to Palestine

The ruins of Stryj's big synagogue

In the Kraków train station she met other rescued people who were checking arriving trains. Jewish survivors helped them and referred them to places where Jewish communities already existed. After three days in Kraków, members of the organization took Donia to the town of Bytom in Silesia. In Bytom she joined the Zionist movement called *Nocham*. She remained in Bytom for a few months. To the best of her memory the American Joint Distribution Committee provided them with food.

On the Way to Palestine

At the end of 1945 all of Donia's group went through the woods to Czechoslovakia and a week later they moved to Laibhaim in Germany. A DP camp was located there and she stayed there for a year. From Laibhaim the whole group went to Rivoli in Italy where they lived at Villa Farazano near the Lago Maggiore.

At the villa Farazano they started to prepare for their *Aliah* (Move to Palestine). The boys unofficially practiced the use of weapons. Yehiel Kadishai, who later became a personal assistant of Prime Minister Menachem Begin, lectured all members of her group.

There was also an educated Lithuanian, a Jewish survivor by the name of Dov Shilansky, who later became a member and speaker for the Israeli *Knesset* (Parliament).

In those days, these apostles were members of the Palestine underground movement. They wanted to give the new immigrants a voice. There were also teachers who taught them the history of the Jewish people. The lectures took place two or three times a week. Among them was a group of young people who were very far away from Judaism. They had spent years in monasteries in the company of nuns. The stories about Israel were strange and wonderful at the same time.

Everyone worked in the kitchen. They had to cook their meals

Donia told me the "ECEL" commander in Italy, (the underground organization that fought against the British) in those days, was Israel Epstein.

One night, in groups of 30 people, they were transferred to Venice and from there by boat to Palestrina Island near Venice, Italy where, far from the prying eyes of the British Intelligence Service, the illegal immigration ship "*Kadima*" was moored. When the small boats carrying the immigrants reached the "*Kadima*," the illegal immigrants boarded quickly thanks to makeshift stairs. The immigrants were ordered to go below deck and to sit on the berths prepared for them. Some of the immigrants were appointed to various tasks such as making sure water was not wasted during the trip.

On the ship there were 794 illegal immigrants from Romania and Poland. There were also some immigrants from Russia, those who defected from the Red Army in order to get to Palestine to participate in the creation of an independent state.

Until almost the very end of war, some of these defectors were fighting the Germans and had reached Berlin during the combat. There by their words, they saw the ruins of the Nazi government buildings. Now they wanted to give all their wartime experiences to the Jewish army that would be established. Their stories raised the morale of the illegal immigrants, mostly survivors who saw in them heroes who partly avenged the terrible injustice done to the Jewish nation. Among the immigrants there were more than one hundred and fifty infants and toddlers.

The ship "*Kadima*"

Everyone gathered on the ship with all their belongings. Since the bunks had no room to store people's meager belongings, they were stored in two warehouses.

On the ship there was a space equipped with several faucets that supplied seawater for washing hands and face. The immigrants were not allowed to use drinking water for washing.

It was early November 1947 as the ship lifted anchor and started the illegal journey to the east. For most of the immigrants, and Donia among them, this was their first time on a ship. Although autumn was in full force, it was very hot below the decks. People felt unwell and there were many who became seasick. Shouts were heard. Nausea and vomiting began. The immigrants were ordered to use special bags prepared in advance in case of vomiting. Often, children had no time to warn an adult that they would soon vomit. The child threw up all over the place.

The special bags weren't always available and the adults began to run to the bathrooms or to the ship's rail. Those who had started vomiting triggered nausea in the others who followed the vomiting pattern. And so it was. When one of the illegal immigrants started making that familiar sound that preceded nausea and vomiting, all those around him were also infected, forcing them to vomit too. The smell was unbearable and those who had not yet been sick joined the vomit chorus. Donia was not spared and she vomited along with everyone.

The illegal immigrants who did not become seasick volunteered as scouts, checking the sky for approaching British aircraft. When the ship pulled slightly away from the coast, the ship's commanders allowed the immigrants to come on deck in order to breathe fresh air that was missing in their bunks below. All of those affected by seasickness lost their appetite and ate almost nothing for most of their journey.

The ship was small. The captain, whose name Donia does not remember, was probably a Greek. He kept the ship quite close to the coast. It sailed along the heel of the boot the Adriatic Sea, the Strait of Tirana and the Ionian Sea. When the small ship was further away from the shore, surveillance was at the discretion of the captain, at the mercy of Heaven and that of the G_d of the Sea: Poseidon.

On board there were Jewish sailors. Nobody knew their real names. If anyone heard any name it was not his real name. In order not to be detected as an illegal immigrant ship by the British aircraft, the ship's commander forbade the illegal immigrants from being on the deck during the day. As darkness fell the volunteers allowed groups of immigrants to come up to the deck to see the evening sky. Some of the immigrants gave up on sleep and sat on deck all night. They slept during the day because they couldn't even hear the word food without triggering nausea. Staying on the deck cured seasickness and nearly stopped the vomiting.

After a few days of sailing the ship commandant announced, "If we cannot break through the British blockade imposed on the shores of our land, we will have to fight them and try to break the siege by force. If we succeed, and it will happen, we must prepare our most important belongings to carry them along quickly. Everyone will be allowed to carry a backpack or a medium sized suitcase that will also be carried on their back because our hands will be busy holding the banister or improvised ladders. Women with babies and small children will disembark using the steps. On the beach trucks belonging to the *Kibbutzim* and villages will wait for us. We will be dispersed among them. If we have to fight the British, then all the immigrants are asked to volunteer. We will fight them using all we have at hand. We have prepared wooden sticks. We will take canned food from the reserve, oil bottles, anything that can be thrown on the heads of the soldiers of his Majesty the King."

The next day, when the shores of the longed for land of Palestine could be seen on the horizon, a reconnaissance plane discovered the "*Kadima.*" It was November 15, 1947.

The ship's route from Italy to Palestine

All adult immigrants came on deck in accordance to the instructions received the day before. The food stockrooms were opened and everyone grabbed what he thought could be used as a weapon against the British soldiers. Babies and small children were left with their mothers and caregivers below deck.

A few hours later two huge destroyers came alongside the ship, one on each side. When the British ships were positioned, there was a call from one of the destroyer's bullhorns not to resist His Majesty the King's Army. The first call was in English and it was well understood by the illegal immigrants. But, just in case, it came again several times in *Yiddish*. No comments were made from the immigrants' side.

The ship increased speed and raced toward the beach. Perhaps she could reach shallow waters and the destroyers wouldn't be able to follow her.

Donia said, "The destroyers were menacing as they approached us. They were twice as tall as our ship. When the destroyers came very close they matched their speed to ours and our ship was almost touched by them. Suddenly we were surprised as ropes were dangled from the destroyer's decks and British soldiers began climbing down. The battle with the British began. A battle we did not have a chance to win. The canned food, which was no longer needed because we had reached our destination, was now hurled at the British soldiers by the immigrants. The sticks prepared in advance were used to beat the British soldiers. The organized fight waned pretty quickly because of the poor condition of the ship. Many infants and children were crying because their parents were busy fighting and not available to comfort them. The battle was lost. As it ended the illegal immigrants sang the *Hatikva* (the Israeli National Anthem). The destroyers escorted the ship to the entrance of the port of Haifa.

A spontaneous decision to hold a hunger strike didn't help. Mothers refused to accept the milk that had been brought from one of the *kibbutzim* for their babies.

"We were expelled from Haifa to Cyprus. A nurse who knew all kinds of tricks gave herself an injection with a needle which resulted in a fever. The British left her in Palestine."

The deportation ship brought them to the port of Famagusta and by trucks they were transferred to "Winter Camp Number 66." Once the immigrants settled down they discovered that the camp was mostly inhabited by the *Betarim* (A right-winged revisionist organization) from Eastern Europe countries so they began to joke. "The British in Cyprus received information from Haifa. The "*Kadima*" illegal immigrants are so very stubborn. They must be *Betarim*. The camp managers understood the directive and put them in Camp 66 which was considered an outpost of the revisionists.

Shortly after they arrived in Cyprus Donia said that they heard about the United Nations November declaration regarding the partition of *Eretz Israel* (Palestine).

"We all danced and were happy because we had a state of our own. The adults among us understood that we were witnessing something happening to our nation after 2000 years. Isreali emissaries told us that soon we will go "home" legitimately. We did a lot of gym exercises and heard lectures from the messengers who came from *Eretz Israel*. They were apparently sent on behalf of a Jewish agency to teach us Judaism and Zionism. Sometimes in the evening we would dance modern dances and during the day we embroidered or did various crafts. We cooked and we had our lives back. We were busy and not bored at all. It was an exciting time.

The Epilogue

Donia's uncle Joseph Heller, who had arranged for Donia's papers, remained in the ghetto with his wife and two children. The connection between Donia and them was completely cut off after the ghetto was closed and sealed. The couple and their two children were murdered when the ghetto was liquidated.

Donia was released from Cyprus after five months. She arrived in Israel just one week after the first Prime Minister David Ben Gurion's declaration of the statehood of Israel.

A little over a year after her arrival in Israel Donia married her fiance Joseph whom she'd met in Cyprus. The wedding took place in Tel Aviv on June 12, 1949. The ceremony was officiated by Rabbi Frankel.

I presented Donia photos of the area around the place where she was born and where her house was. She slowly recognized some of the photos, mostly those of the municipal building in Bolechów and the restored Ukrainian church where she "prayed."

Before the war: the square, municipality
and Ukrainian church in the background

The municipal building in Bolechów today

Once in Israel Malka Rainhartz changed her name to Miriam. She said, "My father was a textile merchant and the owner of a man's clothing atelier where clothes were sewn. Almost all the shops in town belonged to Jews. On Saturdays the shops were closed and the Jews went to the synagogue dressed in their best clothes. They wore prayer shawls. Nobody bothered them or disturbed them along the way. On Sundays, the Christian day of rest, all the shops had to be closed by law. The Jews, whose shops did not bring in enough business during the week, used a discrete side entrance. Usually this door led to their private apartments. Through this door a customer could enter informally, walk through the apartment to the "closed" store, buy what he wanted and leave the same way. Jewish merchants did not heed the law as it was enforced by only one policeman in town, Juzio Bilinski who also spoke *Yiddish* and was willing to accept a gift in return for looking the other way.

About Juzio Bilinski the policeman Miriam said, "Before the war, when the mayor wanted to inform the residents about something, Juzio Bilinski would show up at the town square. He would blow the trumpet that usually hung over his shoulder. People would gather and he would pass along the message from the Mayor.

"The town square information would spread like any other gossip. Printed advertisement or announcement - who could afford such a luxury?

"Jewish children were exempt from school on Saturdays. But they had to prepare and bring to school on Mondays, the work Christian children were required to prepare at home. Jewish children would turn to their Christian friends and get the lessons and guidelines from them. And so it went for many years.

"On national holidays, Independence Day or the day of the Polish Constitution, children from schools would go to churches and synagogue and sing Polish songs of praise and prayed to G_d to take care of Poland."

The hatred of Jews, according to Miriam, was mainly due to envy toward them. The whole area was poor. The farmers were mostly uneducated. They knew only how to cultivate the land

and harvest poor crops. To add to their income they would make brooms, gather berries, fish in the rivers or cut wood for heating. The meager crops, wild fruit found in the forest or the fish they sold to people in town who always had money in their pockets. With the earned pennies they would enter the Jewish store, where at best they would buy something necessary or pay their debt. But they usually would go to a tavern, mostly owned by Jews, buy themselves vodka or any other sort of alcoholic drink and get drunk.

Over the years the Jews tried to save for the future and make a living. The Ukrainians, on the contrary did not care about the future. They played their *Kobzah* (a music instrument) sing songs as in the parable of The Grasshopper and the Ant. These facts they were not aware of or did not want to be aware of.

In addition to the unjustified jealousy, the story of the crucifixion of Jesus by the Jews triggered hatred.

Miriam explained, "Our family, Walik, lived downtown in a new, two storied house. When the Soviet entered in 1939, we had to leave the big, beautiful house which became administrative military offices, the *Wojenkomat*.

"In the German colony in Bolechów lived a Polish Christian named Safczynska. She rented us an apartment and we all moved there.

"In 1940 I married Siumek (Schlomo) Rainhartz. When the Soviets took over in 1939 Siumek had to give up his library which was confiscated. Siumek got a job as an accountant at Shlamp, the German bakery. In 1940 the Soviets expelled the Germans from the German colony back to Germany including the bakery owner, Mr. Shlamp. The bakery was given to the Ukrainian Cooperative management.

"In the first *aktion* in October 1941 no one came to the home of Mrs Safczyńska. No one noticed or knew that Jews were living there. In the winter and spring 1942 there was a terrible famine in the Bolechów area. Some Jews were swollen from eating grass or lost so much weight they became skeletons, almost beyond recognition. Every day ten people died of starvation. In order to survive, Jews sold or exchanged everything they had for food. It was a time when Jews were still allowed to walk around during the day."

In the German colony not far from their house lived a Christian family named Krasnyszyn. Miriam's mother occasionally brought them various objects for sale or to exchange for food.

"In the summer of 1942 as the big *aktion* broke out, Siumek and Malka asked her parents to flee with them into the forest. Malka's mother began to explain that it was *Yom Kippur* Eve (the Jewish New Year) and that the Master of the Universe who saved them when the first *aktion* took place save them once again. Malka's parents did not flee. They stayed at home exactly as in the first *aktion*, sitting at a table in the living room. Unfortunately they didn't know that the neighbor named Krasnyszyn saw them trading objects for food and understood that Mrs. Safczynska had Jewish tenants. He alerted the Germans immediately."

During the great *aktion* on the Jewish New Year of 1942 the Germans took Malka's parents and the rest of the Jews they had rounded up. They were all sent to Bełżec extermination camp.

After the liberation it was one problem after another for the Rainhartzes. Before recuperating from the trauma they just had gone through, Siumek was drafted into the Polish army established in the Soviet Union in an expedited procedure. This was legal because he was a citizen of Poland in the past and would be in the future. Within two days he was on his way to the front.

A few days after Siumek had been drafted, Malka went to Mrs. Safczynska, the woman in the German colony, to see if anything was left behind that belonged to her parents. The woman told Malka what she had already known for two years, who was the man behind the Germans capturing her parents during the big *aktion*. When Malka left the home of Mrs. Safczynska she found herself face to face with the culprit neighbor Krasnyszyn. He laughed in her face like one who says, "Just wait. We will finish you off as well."

Very angry, the next day Malka went to the NKVD town director. "I came to complain about a Ukrainian citizen named Krasnyszyn who betrayed my parents reporting them to the Germans," she said.

"And why did he betray them?" asked the NKVD commander of Bolechów.

"Don't you know what the Germans and their collaborators did here to the Jews?" Malka asked.

Malka was a blonde young woman wrapped in a Ukrainian folk head scarf.

The NKVD commander looked at her thinking she was a typical Ukrainian. He said, "You're lying. You're a Ukrianian yourself. You're not Jewish. You just want to harass someone. I receive such unfound complaints every day. If you want to help the war effort defeat the Facist beast, you have to walk around in the neighboring villages to see where the Banderowci are and tell us. It should be your occupation. We will pay you a salary and you will not have to look for the innocent victims of the population."

This response of the NKVD commander terribly disappointed Malka. She left the office in a sad mood. These are not the Russians who were here in 1939. These apparently also do not like the Jews.

"How can I avenge my parent's murder if the authorities don't want to help?"

Malka learned about the operation *Repatryiacja*, repatriation to Poland from the few remaining local Poles in Bolechów. Those whose conscience was clean did not flee westward, many months before the Red Army returned nor did they escape the hands of murderous Banderowsci or the Ukrainian Rebel Army (UPA).

Malka arrived in Wrocław in early 1945 with the rest of the Bolechów Polish citizens. They reached Wrocław in Western Poland in the new territories taken from Germany and given to Poland according to the Yalta agreements.

A year later Siumek was discharged from the army. He and Malka were reunited. In 1947 Gila, their daughter, was born and they immigrated to Israel and settled in Beersheba. In 1956 they had a son named Samuel.

Malka says that after the liberation in 1944 the mayor of Bolechów was a man named Simkow. (Simków) And not Hucalo as Donia had said.

Some years ago Siumek Rainhartz passed away. Malka told me whatever she remembered following Donia's consent to tell her story.

Maryjka left Bolechów immediately after the liberation and went back to her village near the town of Sambor and was not heard from again.

(Author's note: In the last year I tried to look for Maryjka/ Fridka. She supposedly went to Winnipeg, Canada but I met a dead end and was unable to find her.)

Donia's cousin Isaac Pikholtz was in Russia and survived. Another cousin named Beni Pikholtz was drafted into the Red Army in 1940 and was killed on one of the Fronts. The Soviet War Ministry statement came back, "Lost in battle, his burial place is unknown"

Malka/ Miriam added, "When we were in hiding prior to our release Siumek/Shlomo, my husband, blessed his memory, used to tell me that when we come out, when we are liberated, he would built a palace for Donia for what she did for us. I know she did it with her heart and not to be rewarded. Our paths were separated for a while but here in Israel we met again. She didn't even want a bunch of flowers when we came to visit her.

The Rainhartzes remained grateful to Donia for rescuing them. They wrote about it in the Jewish National Fund Golden Book and planted trees in her name and for her husband Joseph.

The Rainhartz couple kept Donia's request to remain anonymous throughout the years.

To Summarize: "The Bottom Line"

There are many statements in the Jewish language. I will quote two of them which are relevant to the story we just finished reading

One statement says, "THE LUCK OF A GENTILE"

Another statement says, "IT IS DIFFICULT TO BE A JEW"

What is the connection between the two sayings in our story? The relationship is the proof of the two statements being suitable in this case. But how?

198

First proof: If Efrosina Skoblek, alias Donia who saved the Rainhartzes, was a Gentile, she would belong to the appropriate category that says, "The luck of a gentile"

A) She would be recognized as Righteous Among the Nations.

B) As an Israeli citizen she would enjoy a generous cash bonus paid monthly for the rest of her life paid by the state of Israel

Second proof: The fact is that Efrosina Skoblek is in reality a Jewish girl named Dina Pikholtz posing as a Ukrainian. Despite the additional risk she took it upon herself to perform this heroic act "It is difficult to be a Jew" applies fully because due to some parliamentary decision she cannot bear the title of Righteous Among the Nations and consequently receives no title and no grant.

Is not this the proof the two statements are correct?

Dina/Donia today

Dina/Donia with her inseparable
Ukrainian *shalinowa chustka*

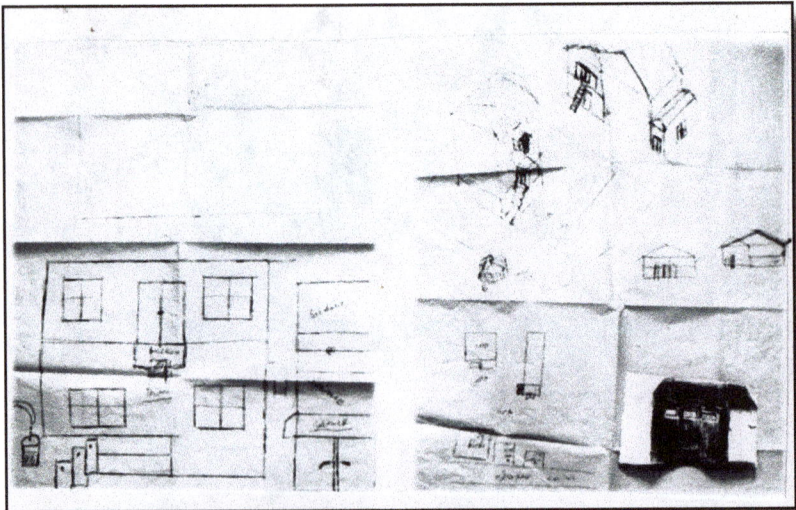

Drawing of the casino area on a piece of gray paper
by Malka Rainhartz when she was in hiding

After my sarcastic criticism toward Yad Vashem and the Parliament's decision, Donia received a nice certificate from B'nai B'rith which is shown below

Yad Vashem honored Dina Ostrower with an invitation
to light one of the six torches
on the eve of Holocaust Remembrance Day.
Her grandson is assisting her.

Dina Ostrower with Israeli President Shimon Peres

Dina Ostrower with
Israeli Prime Minister Benamin Netanyahu

About the Author

Shlomo Adler was born in 1930 in the town of Bolechów in the district of Stanisławów in Poland, to Abraham and Sara Adler. Shlomo had a sister named Miriam who was 6 year older than he. His parents and sister perished in the Holocaust

From the age of six Shlomo studied in a Jewish basic school. In the afternoons he was sent by his parents to the Tarbut school, where he learned Hebrew.

Shlomo and his cousin Juzik (Joseph) Adler, who is one year older than Shlomo, survived the Holocaust. Juzik is the son of Shlomo's father's brother Herman.

After the liberation Shlomo tried to hide his Jewish origin, and for almost two years he pretended to be Polish. He was arrested under accusation of being a Nazi and escaped from Poland. Shlomo's story, *A Jew Again*," may be found on Amazon where it is a best seller.

After ten months in Cyprus, Shlomo arrived Palestine in September 1947. There he lived on a *Kibbutz* and served in the Israeli Army during the War for Independence.

He is married to Ester. They have two sons, Abraham and David. Abraham is married to Malka and David is married to Elana. Shlomo and Ester have five grandchildren; Sarit, Mirit, Koby, Meital and Maya and twin great grandchildren, Shay Li and Matan.

Shlomo worked for ElAl Israel Airlines. He made several improvements in cargo handling and invented and patented a system that increases the capacity in the lower deck of wide body airplanes.

Shlomo lives in Kfar Saba, Israel, He is the head of the Bolechów Descendants in Israel Association. He is currently writing his fourth book, "*From Ashes to Torches.*"

The author's sister Miriam Adler - 1941

The author's cousin Juzik/Joseph Adler - 1948
The two boys, at age thirteen and fourteen, spent a year
in hiding in the loft of a barn during the war.
They were the only members of their family to survive.

Shlomo Adler in 1948

The Adler family in their apartment - December 2013

Shlomo Adler in 2016

www.ingramcontent.com/pod-product-compliance
Lightning Source LLC
Chambersburg PA
CBHW050650270326
41927CB00012B/2951